EVERY SECOND LOST
Marie Harding

CHAPTER 1. MAGGIE

Maggie smiled as she let herself back into the house. It had only been three hours since the funeral and everyone she had spoken to had told her it was too soon to make life changing choices, but she couldn't be happier with her decision. She already felt better for having made a plan, and she was committed to it now, whatever the outcome. It was starting to get dark, so she flicked on the light, poured herself a large glass of red wine and settled on the living room floor next to a pile of her and Daniel's various possessions. Determined to be ruthless she had already taken several boxes of items to the charity shop that morning. The first things she had sorted out were Daniel's clothes. She had emptied his entire wardrobe into bin bags and hauled them down the stairs to the car. His clothes still smelt of him, so they had to go. Now she was left with things that had a sentimental value. Maggie dared not take anything with her that would identify her, so her wedding photos would have to go into storage for a start. She picked up the heavy, silver frame that had stood pride of place on the mantelpiece since the two of them had moved into the house. They looked so happy and carefree back then. Maggie could barely recognise her husband. The man in the photograph was tall and handsome, a picture of health and confidence. He was smiling at something out of sight of the camera. Thinking back, she could not remember the last time she had seen him smile. In recent months he had taken on a haunted appearance. His dark, mahogany skin, dull and lifeless, and he had worry lines etched permanently on his forehead. She turned the picture over and slipped the photograph out of its frame. She carefully folded the picture so it would fit into her handbag and slipped it into the zipped compartment inside. With the picture safely tucked away Maggie moved swiftly through the remaining pile, wrapping each ornament and picture in bubble wrap, and boxing it up ready to go into storage.

Two hours later she finished taping up and labelling the last box. She reached to pour herself another glass of wine, surprised to find the bottle was empty. She opened another from the almost empty rack and sat back in her mother's old armchair to survey her handiwork. In just a few days this room had gone from warm and homely to an empty shell. The walls bore squares of unfaded wallpaper denoting where various pictures and ornaments had hung for many years. Maggie made a note to send a decorator in to brighten the place up before her first rental guests moved in, in just a few days' time. Thinking back, that wallpaper had to have been up there for at least twenty years. She could certainly remember it from her school days. In fact, there was a picture of her and Daniel on their first date that was taken in this very room. He had arrived to take her to prom. She was in a blue, chiffon dress that she still owned. She smiled at the memory.

It was getting late. The streetlights had gone off more than an hour ago. Maggie was light-headed and woozy from the wine. She could barely lift her aching arms, unused to lifting heavy bags and boxes all day. Too tired to get undressed she dragged herself upstairs and flopped onto the mattress that lay on the floor in the spare room. She had not been able to sleep in the bed she shared with Daniel since he died. Despite her tiredness, Maggie couldn't help clicking on the open Facebook tab on her laptop. It popped up to reveal a link to a fundraising page for a three-year-old boy named Freddie, who had just recovered from leukaemia. She had looked at that page many times recently. The picture gallery showed his decline from a chubby faced blonde baby, to a bald and skinny three-year-old. He still had a smile on his face, but it was obscured by the plastic tube inserted in his nose. Thankfully, the boy had just been given the all clear, and his mother was trying to raise £20,000 for some recliner chairs for the hospital to help other parents going through the same ordeal. She had already managed to raise £3000 but it looked like contributions had slowed recently. On a whim, Maggie clicked on the donation button and entered £20,000 in the box. She lingered for a second over the comments box. She desperately wanted to write something but couldn't think of anything appropriate to say. She settled for simply leaving it blank. She watched with satisfaction as the totalizer spun round to the completed position. She hoped the extra money would help make the journey easier for the little boy and his mother.

Maggie had never had children of her own, but she could easily imagine how hard life must have been for Freddie's mother having to cope with watching her child suffer every day. Maggie had been following the boy's progress on his Mother's blog for many months and felt as if she knew them both personally. She knew that Maya was a single mother and was totally devoted to her son. Maggie admired her strength and passion, and secretly believed that the two of them would be good friends if they were ever to meet. Although Maya was careful to never give out her address online there had been several clues that Maggie had been able to follow to work out where she lived. It had been a fun puzzle for her, using photos and snippets of information to work out where they lived. A picture of Freddie getting chemo had revealed the name of the hospital on a nurse's name badge, which gave an approximate location. Maggie had narrowed it down further when Maya had reviewed an independent cupcake bakery on her blog. She googled the bakery website and looked them up on a map. Smallhaven was a little seaside town about fifty miles away on the south coast. A quick search online had produced a lovely flat to rent overlooking the harbour, and as of next week she would be calling it home. Being such a small town, Maggie was certain that once she was living there a chance meeting with Maya would be inevitable.

CHAPTER 2
ALICE 2019

Alice fought back tears as she wrestled her son back into his baby-gro. She dreaded these visits to the local clinic. She knew Alfie was not putting on weight as he should, and she could tell that the other mothers judged her. She tried to keep herself to herself, but everyone knew everyone in this town. She could feel their eyes on her, watching her struggling to do the simple things that they did with ease. She had tried and tried to get Alfie to breast feed, but he just rejected her. No-one else had problems feeding their baby. She felt so useless. Even her own son thought she was not good enough. Wiping her eyes and taking a deep breath, Alice finally popped the last fastener and gathered her squirming child up in her arms. His cheeks were bright red and he screwed his eyes up ready to start crying. She hated resorting to giving him a dummy, as all the books said that babies should learn to self soothe, but she hated him screaming and fussing more. Alice checked that her three-year-old, Lottie, was happy at the toy table with the other toddlers and braced herself for her turn with the health visitor.

The Health Visitor, Margaret was a larger than life character, who always wore brightly coloured clothes with matching accessories. Everything was co-ordinated, from her flamboyant glasses and hair accessories down to her shiny shoes. Alice had known her for years; she had been involved in her first pregnancy and had kept up with the goings on in the family ever since. Alice knew Margaret had a kind heart, but today the gaudy colours and bright smile just served to make her feel grumpy and resentful. She couldn't remember the last time she had the energy to brush her hair, let alone try to find matching jewellery. Her usually healthy-looking honey blonde hair was hanging lank and listless around her shoulders. Her t-shirt was spattered with stains and her jeans hung from her newly skinny body.

"Well Mrs Moretti, how is baby Alfie today? Any luck with the new feeding technique?"

Alice sighed as she took her seat and balanced her son on her knee, removing the dummy and offering him a teether from the bag slung over her shoulder. "I have been trying, but he just doesn't seem to want to take anything from me. I wonder if it's time to just give him a bottle. I'm so tired…"

"Well, he is a little underweight, but you know that breastfeeding is usually the best option for baby. That is literally what your body was designed to do. Think of all those wonderful antibodies you are giving him. And it's good for bonding too." Margaret tickled Alfie under his chin, making him smile and gurgle. "Such a beautiful boy, and so lucky to have his Daddy's colouring." Alice wondered if this was a comment about her own chalky white skin, which she knew had the tendency to enhance the black rings around her eyes. Her husband Benito had gorgeous olive coloured skin, which both of their children had inherited.

"Yes, he's a cutie," agreed Alice. "I just wish he would sleep a little longer." She sighed, jigging the boy up and down on her knee. "I know I shouldn't complain. He's a good boy, but I am tired literally all the time…" Alice could feel tears prickling behind her eyes again. She wondered if she should tell Margaret that she sometimes thought about leaving Alfie in his pushchair outside the shops and just walking home alone. It was not that she didn't love him, she just could not think straight since he had been born. If she could just get some sleep, maybe things would be easier. If Margaret noticed how down Alice was, she didn't react to it. "Don't worry about that Dear. Once he is feeding properly and is not waking up hungry, he will soon be sleeping through the night." Once again Alice wondered if she would be better off just giving him a bottle. Surely, he had enough antibodies by now.

Margaret scribbled something in Alfie's notes then turned her attention to Alice. "How are you doing, Mum?" she asked, without giving her time to answer. "I expect you have been busy at those charity galas I see you at sometimes with that handsome husband of yours. How is Ben by the way? I heard him on the radio yesterday talking about running for mayor. Such a good man, so community minded."

Alice smiled, resigned to the fact that the discussion was well and truly over. She had found yet another fan of Ben, and once that happened there was no way to get the focus of attention back on to her again. Her husband had a way of charming everyone. He took pride in remembering the name of every single person he met. He said it was the reason he was so good at his job. It made people feel special when he could recall their name hours or even weeks later after the briefest of meetings. Appearances were very important to Ben. Alice was suddenly very glad she had not let slip to Margaret how she was feeling. Ben would not be happy for her to be talking about their private problems to everyone. "Oh, you know Ben," She said, forcing a smile, "always busy. The market is booming now, so he is out until all hours showing houses. And the council work takes a lot of his time."

"Even more so once he is Mayor. You can tell him he will be getting my vote." Margaret signed her name in Alfie's record book and handed it back to Alice signalling the end of the appointment. Alice took it and gathered up the now sleeping boy. Once he was settled in the pushchair she headed for the door, collecting Lottie on the way.

Alice fought her way through the automatic doors onto the

street with the double buggy. Her mobile began to ring with Ben's ringtone. She fumbled around in her bag, eventually putting her hand on the phone as the caller hung up. Now Alfie was awake again and starting that high-pitched whining sound that was the precursor to a full-on screaming fit. Lottie, strapped in next to her brother, covered her ears with her chubby little hands and shouted, "make him stop Mummy, make him stop." Deciding against trying to make a call among this chaos, Alice swung around in the opposite direction and headed toward Ben's estate agency in the middle of town. It took only five minutes to walk there, but that was long enough for Alfie to fall back asleep and Lottie to settle down. She was singing a nursery rhyme as they arrived at the door, a picture of angelic goodness. Before Alice could reach for the door handle, one of the agency staff had run around the desk to help her in. There were three young women in the office, and they all made a fuss of the children every time she took them in. Lottie was positively beaming, showing the women the actions to her song, loving the attention she was getting. Alice smiled at the women and left them to it. They were not friends. The women were glamourous. Always well made up and dressed impeccably. They made her feel small.

Ben sat in a glass fronted office at the back of the room. He was pacing around his desk, obviously having a difficult, if muted conversation on the phone. She could see the crease above his nose that he always got when he was angry. As the call ended, he glanced up and saw her. For a fleeting moment she thought she saw a flash of anger cross his features, but she relaxed as he caught the expression and gave her a beaming smile. "I just tried to call you," he said, opening the office door and beckoning her in.

"Yes, that's why I'm here. I was at the clinic and the kids were screaming and the buggy was stuck in the door, and I just thought it was easier to come and talk to you in person." Alice let her shoulders drop and sat heavily on the nearest chair.

"Well, the kids look ok now." Ben reached down for Lottie and swung her up onto his shoulders making her giggle. The three women in the office laughing along with her. Alice rolled her eyes. "Well they are now, but you don't know what it's like sometimes when they both start. I just can't wait for their bedtime today." Ben put Lottie down on the floor and crossed the room to give his wife a hug. "You are doing a great job honey," he said, stroking her arm affectionately. "Isn't she girls?" he continued, addressing the women who were fussing over Lottie. They all agreed with him, telling her at once that she was a great mum, talking over each other in their super sweet, salesperson voices. Alice rolled her eyes again. It was all she could do not to jump up and slap them. She didn't even know their names, but she was pretty sure at least one of them would be called Barbie or Krystal or Mercedes. They were all blonde haired, big lipped and sugary sweet. Ben liked to keep pretty women around him. He was a bit of a pig like that. Alice immediately felt sorry for thinking of them all that way, she was sure the girls were perfectly lovely, but seeing them looking immaculate with their perfect hair and perfect nails just made her feel inadequate. She hadn't showered in three days, let alone had time to get a manicure.

Remembering the phone call, Alice asked Ben what he had called her for. "Just checking you have picked up my jacket from the dry cleaner for the gala tonight," he replied. Of course, she had forgotten about the jacket, and the gala too come to think of it. "About that," she said, looking at him hopefully, "is it really necessary for me to be there? I could use an early night. Plus, I don't have time to sort out the kids and get ready. My hair is a mess..." She trailed off. Too tired to even list the reasons why she didn't want to drag herself out that evening. She hated those charity things at the best of times, but now Ben was running for Mayor they got stuck talking to everyone in the room. Occasionally she would be lucky and manage to hide out in a corner, avoiding eye contact, but since Ben had started running for Mayor the fight was becoming intense and she would find herself stuck in boring conversations with dull people. She couldn't think of anything she would like to do less. Ben lowered his voice and painted his face with a tight smile. "Alice, you know this is important to me," he said, sounding dangerous. "How would it look if I were to turn up alone? I need you to support me on this."

Alice knew when she was fighting a losing battle. "Ok," she said with a sigh, "but I still don't have time to go to the dry cleaner. Can't you just wear the blue suit instead?" Ben let his breath out slowly as if counting in his head. "I want to wear the black suit," he said, barely controlling his anger now. "I told you that a week ago. You have had a whole week to go to the dry cleaners. It's not as if you have anything else to do all day." One of the office girls, Alice thought it might be Krystal, butted into the conversation that she had obviously been listening in on. "Hey Benny, give her a break. It's hard looking after two children all day. Besides, you look hot in the blue suit anyway." She gave him a flirty smile and walked away. Ben grinned at the obvious flattery. "Fine. I'll wear the blue suit this time," he agreed.

After saying their goodbyes, Ben walked Alice out. When they were safely out of earshot, he turned to face his wife, grabbing her upper arm, and holding her tightly. "I don't appreciate you embarrassing me like that." Alice shook her head, two lines appearing at the bridge of her nose as her face creased in confusion "What do you mean? What was embarrassing?" She asked, genuinely confused. "You come in, looking like something the dog dragged in, complaining you are tired," said Ben, angling himself away from the shop window so none of the women inside could see his angry face. "Why can't you look after yourself for god's sake? Would it hurt to run a comb through your hair every now and again? And look at the state of the kids," he continued, gesturing toward the children. "Lottie has food on her dress." He shook his head in disappointment. "I expect more from you."

Alice dropped her head. Tears welling in her eyes again, threatening to spill over. "I'm sorry. I will try harder. I'm just so tired right now. Alfie keeps me awake all the time." She stared at the floor, trying to compose her face before anyone could see what a mess she was. "Yeah, yeah. I know the excuses," said Ben shaking his head. "I will be home in a couple of hours. And don't worry about coming to the gala tonight, I can't take you out looking like that." Ben turned abruptly and strode back into the shop without a backward glance. As she left, Alice could already hear the girls back in the office laughing at some joke he had made. No doubt they were laughing at her. Why was she such a failure at everything?

CHAPTER 3
MAYA 2019

Maya let herself into her parent's house to the sound of quiet snores coming from the lounge. She stepped quietly into the room and stood for a minute watching her son sleeping soundly, nestled on the lap of his Grandad, who was the source of the sound. Not wanting to wake the snoozing pair she wandered down the hall to the kitchen to make a cup of tea. "Hello Love," greeted her mum cheerfully from her spot by the window overlooking the sandy bay. The sun was starting to set behind the low clouds scattering honey highlights across the sea. "Hi Mum. How was Freddie today?" Maya asked, flicking the kettle on.

"He was a darling, as usual. You don't need to worry," Pamela said, taking two mugs from the tree and standing them on the counter beside the kettle. "He was fine. We had a great time." Maya smiled and stepped over to hug her mother. Freddie had only been given the all clear from his cancer a few months ago, and she was not yet used to leaving him with anyone else. She trusted her parents completely, but she had checked her phone every five minutes the whole day, worried that something may have happened. "That's great. He loves the zoo." Maya smiled heaping sugar into her mug as the tea brewed. She joined Pamela at the window blowing the hot tea to cool it. The phone in her pocket pinged with a new notification. Maya pulled it out and scrolled through her messages letting out a small yelp, her hand flying up to cover her mouth. Pamela almost dropped her tea in a panic, immediately assuming something was wrong. "What on earth is the matter?" she demanded, registering the way

Maya's face was set in shock. "What's happened?" Maya shook her head, her eyes wide. She was visibly trembling.

"Let me see." Pamela reached for the phone and Maya turned it so she could see the screen. "Look at the total Mum. We have the money. All of it. I can't believe it"

Pamela looked at her in confusion. "What do you mean you have all of it. There was only £3000 in there this morning. You can't have raised £17000 in one afternoon."

"Well it's there. All of it. I'm telling you. The whole lot, I swear to god." Maya pointed at the screen again, using two fingers to enlarge the total on the screen. "Someone donated twenty grand today. Holy fuck." She shook her head in disbelief.

Maya's happiness was infectious. Pamela couldn't remember the last time she had seen her daughter this happy. "Come on. Let's wake your Dad. This calls for a celebration. I have champagne in the fridge!"

Maya hugged her mum and spun her around. "I can't believe it. Think of the difference that money will make. I'll get the glasses"

Maya practically skipped over to the fridge to grab the champagne. She gathered three glasses and a juice box for Freddie, who she could hear was now wide awake and talking a mile a minute. She joined the others in the lounge and poured drinks for everyone. Once they had made a toast, she picked up her phone to look again at the total to make sure she had not imagined it. She hadn't noticed before, but the donor had left their name. "Do either of you know a Maggie Taylor?" she asked. Graham shook his head no, but Maya noticed Pamela's face blanch as she tightened her grip on the champagne glass. "Do you know her Mum? Who is she?" Pamela regained her composure. She shook her hair and brushed her hand through it, as though she were trying to dislodge a stubborn memory.

"Oh, no one, I mean I don't know. I thought I knew the name, but I don't." She took a large glug of her champagne, draining the glass, and reached it out for a top up. "Fill me up please darling. This is good stuff." She paused. "I just wonder, are we sure we should be taking this person's money, this Maggie? I mean, we don't know her. She could be a stalker.... or, or a serial killer or something."

Graham frowned at his wife. "What are you talking about? Serial killers don't donate thousands of pounds to charity. Of course we are taking the money." He shook his head and turned to Freddie, hugging him close and kissing him on the forehead, which caused the boy to wriggle away laughing, wiping the kiss off with his sleeve. "This is for the kids Pamela," he said, in his best no-nonsense tone. "Anyone who wants to help little angels like our Freddie is alright with me."

"Yes, of course we should take the money," Pamela said, trying to downplay her reaction. "But I just think you can't be too careful you know. There's a lot of strange people around." Maya leaned over and put an arm around her mum's shoulders. "Ok Mum. We will be careful. But let's just enjoy this shall we? If a stranger wants to give us some money that's great. You know what difference it will make to other families like us. This can only be a good thing." Unwilling to make any more fuss Pamela agreed to forget it and continued with the celebrations. She couldn't let them see how rattled she was to see Maggie's name pop up like that. What did it mean? It couldn't be a coincidence that she had chosen Freddie's appeal to donate to. She wondered what the true cost of this money was going to be. She would protect this family in every way she knew how. She just hoped she wouldn't need to.

CHAPTER 4
MAGGIE 2019

Maggie opened the blinds and looked out over the peaceful river, watching a cormorant dive for its breakfast. She was glad she had made the decision to move. This town was everything that her old life was not. Although it was late September and the evenings were getting shorter, the weather was still beautiful. She was renting a spacious three bedroom flat overlooking the river, with views right across the neighbouring fields to the sea. She didn't need a space that big but had fallen in love with the view as soon as she had arrived. She had not even bothered to look at any other properties. Her favourite feature was a huge wraparound balcony that could be accessed from either the living room or the master bedroom. Maggie had taken to having her morning coffee out there and watching the sun rise. The place was so peaceful, she barely heard any road noise. Instead she had had to get used to the sound of the rigging on boats in the harbour rattling in the wind, and the occasional shriek of one of the resident seagulls. She was not sure what type they were yet. Only that they were huge and always hungry, and not well liked by the locals.

Today she had decided to venture into town and wander around the shops. There was a large shopping centre, for what appeared to be a very small village. Until now she had been enjoying sampling the wares of the local fast-food establishments, but she supposed it was about time she bought some vegetables. She dressed quickly and drove a few short minutes to the local supermarket, groaning when she saw how large the car park was. This was not going to be the small, local shopping experience she had hoped for. Maggie took a trolley from the nearest bay and headed toward the entrance. To Maggie's relief, the shop was almost empty. She still struggled with the occasional panic attack from time to time and crowded supermarkets were a trigger for her. She wandered the aisles for a few minutes, happily picking up anything that looked good to her. She had not been shopping for what seemed like years. It used to be her favourite thing to do but she had got out of the habit, finding it easier to shop online and avoid people altogether. No-one knew her here, so she was free to browse as long as she wanted.

After a contented ten minutes, Maggie became aware of a shrieking child, whose heart-wrenching screams seemed to travel the extent of the supermarket. She turned her trolley around and headed toward the sound, almost immediately bumping into a tired looking blonde-haired woman with two small children. The source of the noise was the little girl, who looked to be aged about three. She had turned herself a violent shade of red with her screaming, which seemed to have caused her younger brother to join her in sympathy. Maggie could see that the Mother was barely holding it together. She was shaking and looked to be on the edge of tears. Maggie palmed her lucky crystal that she kept in her pocket and knelt on the floor in front of the screaming girl. She held out two fists. "Pick one," she said, smiling to get the girl's attention. The screaming subsided, but the girl looked at her wearily. "Pick one." The girl was interested now and reached out a shaky hand to point at Maggie's right hand. She had stopped crying now and was watching Maggie with fascination. Her little brother was also starting to calm down, much to the relief of the Mother. Maggie opened her hand to reveal the shiny, pink coloured quartz heart. The handed it to the little girl who took it with a look of wonder on her face. "This is a lucky heart," she said to the little girl, who had stopped crying and was fascinated by Maggie. "You keep it in your pocket, and it keeps you safe," she explained. "My name is Maggie. What's your name?"

"Lottie is my name. My brother is Alfie," said the little girl, smiling now. "Pleased to meet you Lottie," replied Maggie, standing back up and turning her attention to the children's mother. She thought she recognised her vaguely. Maybe she had seen her around the town. Maggie offered her hand to the pretty woman with a smile. "Hi, I'm Maggie. You must be Lottie's mum."

"Alice. Sorry about that, she is such a headstrong girl, I just can't cope sometimes," Alice dropped her head, her eyes brimming with tears. "Who am I kidding?" she continued, forlorn. "It's more than sometimes. Since Alfie was born, I have just been useless. I am a bad mother, they deserve more..." She wiped tears from her eyes with her sleeve, ashamed and embarrassed to have shared so much information to a stranger. Maggie fished in her handbag and produced a pack of tissues and moved in to give Alice a hug. She was in full flow now, her shoulders shaking with silent sobs, and her face puffy from crying, but Maggie was sure now that she did recognise her. She had seen her on Maya's Facebook page. She had been pictured with Maya at an award ceremony or gala of some sort. She looked a lot more glamourous and confident in the pictures, but Maggie was sure it was the same person. "Hey, let's get a coffee and have a proper chat," she suggested. "I noticed a coffeeshop on the way in."

Alice nodded from behind the tissue. Maggie left her half-filled trolley where it was in the aisle and steered Alice and her double buggy toward the coffee shop at the front of the store. Once they were seated and Lottie was occupied with colouring pencils from the counter and Alfie was working on a biscuit, Maggie turned her attention to Alice. "I got you a double shot latte. You looked like you could use the caffeine." Alice took the proffered mug and added a generous helping of sugar. "I'm so embarrassed. What must you think of me? I'm so rubbish" She stirred her coffee slowly while dabbing at her eyes with the napkin. "Do you have children?" she asked. "I don't even know you and you are already better with my kids than I am." She let out a shaky breath. Tears once again threatening to overwhelm her.

"Nonsense. I'm sure you are doing a great job as a Mother, and no, I don't have any children. Your kids are clean and healthy, and you clearly love them. What more could they need? Here, try some of this cake, it's guaranteed to make you feel better." Maggie slid a slice of chocolate cake and a fork across the table toward Alice. She was so thin and pale Maggie wondered when she had last eaten a decent sized meal. The two women spent a pleasant half an hour chatting and getting to know each other. Lottie was delighted with her new stone and kept turning it over and over, watching the light play on the crystal.

Alice glanced at her watch and gasped. "Oh, it's getting late. I must get home and make dinner and get these two sorted for bed. Ben will be cross if I am late again." She tidied the plates on the table into a pile and lifted Alfie out of his highchair. "Thank you for this Maggie, really. And I'm so sorry for causing a scene earlier."

"Anytime," smiled Maggie. "Your kids are delightful, and it was nice to meet a new friend. I don't know anyone in the town yet. Maybe we can do this again?" Maggie raised her eyebrows to Alice in a question as she helped Lottie into her cardigan and lifted her off the chair and into the waiting buggy.

"That would be great," Alice smiled. "I could show you around the town." Maggie grabbed one of the pencils Lottie had been playing with, wrote her number on a napkin and passed it to Alice. "Just call me. Anytime is fine. Honestly"

Alice smiled and nodded as she steered the heavy buggy with her basket of shopping toward the checkout. Maggie couldn't be bothered to finish her shopping now, so she followed her new friend out to the car park and helped her load the kids into her car. She had only got halfway to her own car before she heard Alice calling to her. She turned to find her new friend running toward her, once again in a state of panic. "My car won't start.

Can you believe the day I'm having? Can you just wait with the kids for two minutes while I call the AA? I can't handle it if they start screaming while I am on the phone. And today of all days when I am already running late."

Maggie looked from Alice to her car, and back. "How about I just take drive you home for now and tomorrow I can pick you up and bring you back to wait for the AA."

"Really?" Alice said, letting her shoulders drop in relief. "Oh, that would be amazing. Thank you so much, you are a lifesaver." She looked at Maggie in awe. "Honestly, where did you come from?" she laughed.

"It's entirely my pleasure. Don't worry about it. Wait here, I will go and get the car." Maggie smiled to herself as she half jogged back to her car. Of all the people to bump into. Her first trip out in Smallhaven and she hits it off with a Maya's oldest friend. She hadn't even had to try. Maggie returned a couple of minutes later and leant into the back of Alice's car to unbuckle the now sleeping Alfie. He was a gorgeous boy. Rosy red cheeks and silky blonde hair. His eye lashes were clumped together with the remnants of his tears. Maggie bent down to kiss him and smoothed his curls back out of his eyes. Lottie had already clambered out of her seat and was asking a hundred questions a minute in her excitement. Maggie held her chubby little hand to keep her out of the way of the passing cars, while Alice loaded the buggy and her shopping into the boot. Alice opened the back door of Maggie's car to help the children in. "You have car seats. I didn't think you had children. Why do you have car seats?" Embarrassed at her brashness, she lowered her voice. Cross with herself for coming across rude. "Sorry, I'm glad obviously, but just surprised. I'll shut up now"

Maggie smiled reassuringly at her. "I have two baby nieces. I keep the seats in the car for them. I forgot they were there to be honest." To save Alice any further embarrassment she quickly strapped the two children in, and they set off for Alice's home.

"I don't know my way around town yet. You will have to direct me" This was not entirely true. Maggie had already acquainted herself with the whereabouts of Maya's house on her first night in town and knew several different routes between there and her apartment already. However, Alice lived on the other side of town in a big modern estate. Maggie was impressed by the gates as they drove up the driveway. She had never known anyone who had a gatekeeper before. When she said as much to Alice she laughed. "Oh, don't be impressed. This isn't all ours. It's all just for show. You will find everything in this estate is. All false smiles and garden parties." She rolled her eyes and fished around in her handbag for her keys. "I can't stand it, but Ben loves it."

"Is Ben your husband?" Maggie asked, following Alice's directions as she pointed left and right around the maze of identical looking roads. "Uh huh," nodded Alice. "Benito Moretti. We have been together since he found me my first flat four years ago. He's Italian, and a beautiful looking man, if I say so myself." She pointed out the house. "It's the next one on the right. Number four. You can pull in front of the garage. That's my usual spot. If you park in Ben's space, there is a good chance he will not even notice you and just drive your car straight through the wall." She undid her seatbelt as they drew to a halt.

Maggie laughed and parked where Alice had indicated. Together, the two women unloaded the car of its passengers and carried the shopping into the house. Alice showed Maggie through to the children's playroom, which was conveniently located next to the kitchen. Maggie laid the sleeping boy down on the sofa and propped pillows around him, so he didn't fall off, while Alice turned on the tv and handed Lottie a carton of juice. "I have to get the dinner on, you're welcome to stay."

"Thanks, but I have to run a few errands." Maggie stood, getting ready to leave. "At least stay for a cup of tea. Ten minutes," persuaded Alice. Maggie could tell that her new friend was not going to let her go easily, so she agreed to the tea and settled down on the sofa with Lottie who had found a book and was urging Maggie to read it to her. Maggie gladly took the book and Lottie clambered up on to her lap and settled down with her thumb in her mouth. Maggie felt tears prick her eyes as she softly stroked Lottie's curls away from her forehead. Alice pulled up a side table beside them and placed Maggie's mug of tea on it. "You're a natural at this. She doesn't usually take to strangers," she said, putting a hand on Maggie's shoulder.

Both women jumped at the sound of the front door slamming. Neither of them had heard a car or anyone approach. Alice hurried toward the door and Maggie turned to see what was happening. A tall, olive skinned man was standing in the hall with a face like thunder. Maggie supposed this must be the husband, Ben. She could hear Alice whispering frantically to him. She couldn't hear what was being said, but guessed it was about her when he turned to stare in her direction. The minute his eyes caught hers, Ben dropped the angry look and a smile spread across his face, highlighting his beautiful cheekbones. Maggie had to agree with Alice that he was a striking looking man. He strode, confidently toward her with his hand outstretched, all charm and welcome. Maggie could barely believe this was the same man who had looked so angry mere seconds ago. She shook his hand and introduced herself. Ben perched himself on the arm of the sofa Maggie was sitting on, leaning over her to kiss Lottie on the head.

"I can see you have met my angels, Maggie. they seem to like you. That's a good enough recommendation for me. I have been telling Alice for ages we should get a Nanny to help her out. She needs all the help she can get at the moment." Maggie caught Alice's eye, before she quickly dropped her gaze to the floor and turned around. "The children are great. I'm sure Alice is doing a fine job. It's not easy having two under four-year olds..." Ben stood up, half turned toward his wife. "She wouldn't let me hire you anyway. She always says she wouldn't want a hot nanny. She gets terribly jealous you know."

Maggie didn't know what to say, so she turned back to the book and began reading it out aloud once more to Lottie, who had begun to stir on her lap. Ben made her uncomfortable. He was perfectly charming, but there was an edge to him that made her skin crawl. Maggie wondered if she would always distrust men now. Had this become her default position, to feel suspicious all the time? She felt like she was always on the look-out for a hidden motive. She felt sad that her mind always jumped to the worst possible scenario, but she had seen enough and been lied to often enough to know that people are not always honest. She resolved in her head to try to be more trusting and not read into the situation based on her own circumstances. She would not judge Ben based on that one small interaction. He had just got home from work and was clearly tired and irritable. She would give him another chance. "So, Ben, what is it that you do?" she asked, knowing the answer already but wanting to start a topic that she knew he would find easy to talk about.

"I own Moretti's estate agency in town," he said, with a note of pride in his voice. Maggie lifted a now sleeping Lottie in her arms and stood to lay her down on the sofa. "Sounds like a restaurant or a posh Ice Cream parlour" she said with a grin.

"Actually, he is the best Estate Agent in town," Alice called over from the kitchen area, where she was currently cooking a delicious smelling pasta sauce. "He sold me my first flat. Did I tell you that?"

Maggie perched on the opposite arm of the sofa to Ben and folded her arms. "Actually, you did," she said to Alice, before directing her questions back to Ben. "Maybe you could look out for a house for me. I'm renting a lovely flat, but I didn't want to buy until I worked out where the nice areas of town are. Sounds like you are the very man to help."

"I have an idea," Ben sent a charming smile across to Maggie "Why doesn't Alice show you around town? You can see for yourself what the place has to offer. She would be a better guide than me."

Alice looked up from her cooking, clearly surprised. "Yeah, let's do that. I could do that. I would love to show you around."

Maggie stood up and grabbed her handbag from the table where she had left it when she came in, grabbing hold of her car keys. "How about tomorrow morning I drive you to your car and once its fixed you can start by showing me where I can get a decent cup of tea?" She suggested to Alice.

"That sounds great," Ben answered for her. "There's no need to rush off. Why don't you stay and eat? Moretti's has the best pasta chef in town." He smiled at his wife.

Alice wiped her hands on her apron and reached for the olive oil on the shelf above her. "There's plenty to go around, you are most welcome."

"Thanks, but not tonight. I would love to another time though. How about I pick you up tomorrow at 9ish and we can take it from there?" She approached Alice and gave her a hug and a quick peck on the cheek.

"That's great. We will be ready and waiting," Alice smiled as Ben stood and escorted Maggie to the door, leading her with a hand on her shoulder blade.

"Say bye to the kids for me," she said to him as she walked through the door, keen to remove herself from him, still able to feel his sweaty palm on her back, making her skin crawl.

CHAPTER 5
ALICE 2019

Alice waited until Ben had closed the door behind Maggie before she turned back toward the kitchen. Ben had surprised her by encouraging her to show Maggie around. He knew how busy she was with the house and the kids and he usually avoided bringing strangers into the house. She had been pleased to think that Maggie wanted to spend time with her, but she was quickly starting to doubt her decision. What did she have to offer someone like Maggie? She resolved to speak to her while they were waiting for the AA the next morning and tell her she was too busy for a new friend right now. She looked around her. Both children were asleep, fully clothed on the playroom sofas, her shopping was strewn across the kitchen floor, still in the carrier bags and there were pots and pans and empty packets littering the worktops from her rushed meal preparation. She turned down the heat on the pot of spaghetti that was threatening to boil over and began tidying as best she could whilst finishing the pasta sauce. Where was Ben? Five minutes ago, he had been the attentive husband, and now that she could use a hand he was nowhere to be seen. She called up the stairs for him to give her a hand. Without waiting for a reply, she returned to the playroom and woke Lottie, sitting her in her highchair at the kitchen table and occupying her with a chunk of garlic bread while she woke Alfie. Once both children were settled Alice dished them up portions of Bolognese, using her little blender to puree Alfie's before spoon-feeding him at the table.

Alfie fidgeted and cried in his seat. Several times he turned his head as she got the spoon to his mouth, causing her to smear the orange-coloured paste over his face. She wiped him with a wet wipe, which caused him to fuss even more and push the spoon away. This was not like him. He usually had a healthy appetite and loved his meals. She put her hand on his forehead, worried that he may have a temperature. She gave up trying to get him to eat the pasta and instead fetched yoghurts from the fridge for him and his sister. Alfie still refused to eat and had now settled into a continuous whine. Frustrated, she called once again for her husband. "Ben, can you come down here and help me for a minute please?" He was always disappearing when she needed him most. She lifted Alfie out of his chair and was helping Lottie down from the table when Ben appeared, hair still wet from the shower. "Oh good, you're here. Can you help me with the kids? I'm running behind today, and I think Alfie is coming down with something."

"I've been at work all day. And I'm tired." Ben sat down at the table and pulled up a game on his phone. "It's not my fault you are running behind. You didn't seem worried about that when you were inviting strangers in for dinner"

"Maggie gave me a lift home as my car wouldn't start. And you were the one who invited her to stay and eat. I thought you liked her," Alice shook her head. "Lottie, its bedtime, go kiss Daddy goodnight." The little girl let go of her mum's hand and skipped over to her Dad, climbing up on to his lap for a kiss. He pecked her cheek and rubbed her head absent-mindedly, without ever taking his eyes off his game. "Night night, Princess. See you to-morrow." Alice sighed and led Lottie up to the stairs. "I will be ten minutes Ben. Could you please serve up? I'm starving"

Ben sat upright and slammed his phone down on to the table, startling Lottie and making Alfie cry. "For god's sake Alice. Why are you making dinner? We have that fundraising gala tonight. Are you planning to eat two meals?"

Alice felt like she was about to cry. She had forgotten about the bloody gala and hadn't he just invited Maggie to stay? He knew she was cooking dinner. She couldn't face spending yet another evening pretending to be cheerful and watching as Ben flirted with every pretty woman in the room. She didn't know why he insisted on taking her to these things. He didn't need her. As soon as they arrived, he would leave her standing by the bar while he worked his way around the room, chatting to everyone, oblivious to her.

"I think I should stay home tonight." Alice glanced furtively at Ben to see what reaction her words had elicited. "Alfie needs me. And I have lots to do here. You don't need me to be there…"

"You are my wife. What do you think it looks like if I turn up without my wife?" Ben's voice raised a little higher. "Have you forgotten I'm running for Mayor? I don't need people asking questions about my personal life and wondering why I don't have a wife who supports me. How does that look? Huh?"

Ben was shouting now, and the children had started to whimper in her arms. "Sorry. I'm sorry. Let me just put Lottie to bed and I will get ready. Can you just watch Alfie for me? Hayley will be here any minute. I understand, really, I do. "

Placated, Ben grunted and turned back to his game. "And for god's sake try to make an effort. You look a bloody mess." Alice put Alfie down on the sofa next to his Dad. Lottie scrambled up onto his lap for a kiss, which he bestowed without paying any attention to her. Once Alice had settled Lottie down, she jumped quickly into the shower. She knew she should try, but she was just so exhausted. In her head she went through her wardrobe options and decided to settle on her favourite black dress. She was still carrying some extra weight from Alfie and she knew it covered all her lumps and bumps. She rough dried her hair with some mousse and let it fall into its natural curls. A few minutes later, once she had applied make up for the first time in about a year, she gave herself an appraising look in the mirror. She would pass.

Alice could tell Ben was angry before he even said a word. As she came down the stairs, she could hear him pacing up and down the room and he wasn't even trying to calm down Alfie, who was now bright red and screaming at the top of his lungs from the sofa. She crossed the room quickly and scooped the screaming infant into her arms, reaching for a wipe to clean his hot, little face.

"That was Hayley on the phone," Ben spat at her. "It's a bit convenient that she cancelled at the last minute, just when you don't want to go out, don't you think?" Alice was confused but knew better than to argue. "That's a pretty shitty way of getting out of it, Alice"

"I don't know what you are talking about. I haven't even spoken to Hayley. I didn't even hear the phone; I had the hairdryer on. "

Ben grunted at her and turned his back, continuing to pace. Alice thought fast. "Ok, look. Why don't I see if Maggie can come back and watch the kids? She said she was happy to help. How about I give her a call?"

"Fine. Whatever." Ben walked away, leaving Alice to make the call. Twenty minutes later Alice checked on Alfie one last time. The Calpol she had given him earlier had taken his temperature down, but she still felt bad to be leaving him. There was a knock at the door, and she heard Ben open it and greet Maggie. He was using his work voice and was all charm. Even without looking she knew he would have his most polished smile on his face. Maggie giggled at something he said. He had always had a way of making people trust him. A twinkle in his eye and a way of listening to someone that made them feel like they were the   only person in the room. She had seen him charm his way around a room hundreds of times and was jealous of his ease and confidence. She was always plagued with self-doubt. His complete social opposite. She knew that when they were together people questioned what he saw in her. With a last quick look at Alfie, Alice left the room, pulling the door to behind her. She grabbed her clutch bag from the landing shelf where she had left it and made her way down to Ben and Maggie.

"Here's my beautiful wife," Ben held out his hand for her to take as she reached the bottom stair. "Would you even know that a body like that could have had two babies?"

"You do look gorgeous Alice," agreed Maggie. "I love that dress on you. It really brings out your eyes."

Alice smiled at the compliment and took hold of Maggie's elbow to show her into the kitchen, where she had prepared a list of instructions and emergency numbers. Maggie took it all in her stride, nodding at the appropriate places and agreeing where she should. She could tell Alice was anxious about leaving her children and wanted to make her feel as comfortable as she could. "Really Alice, it's fine. Go and have a good time. I've got this"

"Ok. But you must promise to call me if anything happens at all ok? Me, not Ben. Call me. Ok?" Alice said, with a worried look on her face.

Maggie agreed and resorted to leading Alice back out to the door and her waiting husband. Ben smiled as he ushered Alice outside to the waiting cab, one hand on the small of her back, the image of a gentleman.

The taxi pulled up outside the hotel twenty minutes later. Ben was on top form and Alice had cheered up considerably to the point that she was almost looking forward to the evening. Ben got out of the car and walked around to help her out. They walked hand in hand up to the door and were shown toward their table. Alice was delighted to see that they had been seated with her best friend Maya and her parents Pamela and Graham. She only recognised one other person at the table, Oliver Anderson, who was a teacher at the local secondary school. Maya introduced her and Ben to everyone, and Alice immediately forgot everyone's name, safe in the knowledge that Ben would remember everyone for her.

"Alice, you look stunning, you yummy mummy you," said Maya, standing up to give her friend a kiss hello. "And Ben, you are your usual gorgeous self," she continued, giving Ben a hug. When she pulled away Alice noticed him giving Maya an appraising look, his eyes hovering a moment too long on her cleavage. She did her best to ignore it, not wanting to start an argument. "You look amazing, as ever, Miss Young" said Ben, giving Maya a kiss on the hand. She blushed and returned his smile as he continued around the table saying his hellos to everyone. He seemed to know everyone, not just at their table, but in the entire room, and everyone seemed to love him. Everyone apart from Oliver that was. He seemed to be looking at Ben as if he were a piece of gum on the bottom of his shoe.

Alice found herself sat with Oliver and Maya's parents on one side of her, with Ben and Maya on the other. She had hoped to be sat next to Maya so the two of them could spend the evening people watching and gossiping. As it was Ben monopolized the conversation with Maya, so Alice was forced to try to talk to the very shy figure of Oliver. It was either that or be sat on her own, not talking to anyone, like the sad loner she was.

The food was delicious, and no-one was particularly inclined to speak while they were eating, which helped Alice out. She was trying every trick in the book to get Oliver to talk to her, but without much success. She resorted to talking about her children, trying to make him laugh with stories of the funny things Lottie had said recently. The only time she managed to get him to appear interested in talking was when she spoke about Maya and Freddie. It seemed he had been following the boy's progress on Maya's blog, and was as excited as she had been to hear that the total amount of the target had been raised. Alice was touched by how much Oliver seemed to care about her friends. She knew that Maya had fallen out with Oliver a while back, but she couldn't remember why. She made a mental note to ask her when they were next alone.

Now that she had broken the ice with Oliver, the conversation – and the wine – was flowing. Alice forgot about being tired and started to let her hair down. This was the first time she had been out since having Alfie and she was starting to enjoy herself. After dinner she took to the dancefloor with Maya, where they danced and chatted to one another as if there was no-one else in the room. It felt to Alice like it had when they had first gone clubbing together. Maya had always attracted a lot of male attention with her hourglass figure and shimmering blonde hair, and nothing had changed. It seemed to Alice that all eyes were on Maya, including Ben's. She noticed that he rarely looked away from her. Even when he was speaking to someone else, she could see him gazing in Maya's direction, as though mesmerized by her. In the past Alice would have been jealous and angry, and would have confronted Ben about it, causing a row that could rumble on for days afterward. Now, however, she was interested to note that she was indifferent to it. She couldn't bring herself to care who he was looking at. The old suspicions and worries she had about his fidelity and loyalty seemed trivial and unimportant. Alice helped herself to another glass of champagne from a circulating waiter and drank it down, returning to the dancefloor, where she could pretend just for tonight that she was eighteen again and life was simple and uncomplicated.

CHAPTER 6
MAYA 2015

Maya was a couple of minutes early so she did a quick make up check in her reflection in the glass of the front door before ringing the bell. She liked to make a good first impression. The door was opened by a young teenage boy carrying a guitar in a case like a backpack. "You can go and sit in the front room and wait. Oliver is just doing something upstairs for a minute." He edged past Maya without even looking at her and continued down the path to the street. Maya did as she was told, shutting the door behind her, and making her way to the front room. It was a huge old house with squeaky wooden floorboards. The front room was painted a gloomy shade of blue with a white marble fireplace dominating one wall. In contrast the rest of the room was full of high-tech sound recording equipment. There were guitars and keyboards lined up against one wall and a full electronic drum kit stood in the corner behind a console covered in buttons and knobs that Maya knew was some sort of recording desk. There was a squashy leather sofa in the opposite corner. In the middle of the room stood several stools with microphones in front of them. Maya walked around the room, taking everything in, before settling on one of the stools.

"Ah, you must be Maya. Jason let you in I suppose. Thanks for waiting." A tall, slender man with unruly hair thrust his hand toward her to shake. "I'm Oliver. I understand we are going to be doing some voice coaching?" He sat down at the keyboard and Maya swivelled on her stool to see him. He was smiling at her expectantly.

"I have an audition for stage school in a few months," she began, "I need to get in there. That's my best chance for getting my big break. I want to be in musicals, in the West End. It's my dream to play Eponine in Les Mis. I love that show so much." Maya caught Oliver taking a quick peek at his watch and stopped herself. She was starting to babble. She always did that when she was nervous, she found it hard to stop talking once she started. "Ok then," said Oliver, shuffling around in a box of sheet music next to him. "Let's see what you can do, Eponine. I assume you know "On My Own?" He arranged the music on his stand and motioned for Maya to stand alongside him so she could follow the words and started playing the intro while she prepared herself.

Maya loved nothing more than to sing her heart out. She put everything she could into the performance, pretending to herself that she was onstage giving an audition. Oliver matched his timing to her singing perfectly. It felt as though he were reading her mind, slowing when she slowed and adapting the volume to meet the intensity of her vocals. She felt as though the two of them could read each other's minds. As the song drew to a close Oliver sat back and let his hands rest on his lap. Maya smiled at him expectantly, waiting for an assessment.

"Well," said Oliver, "you certainly have a good set of lungs. That was impressive for someone with no previous training. We could work on your breathing and your pronunciation to start with." Maya nodded. She was ready to work as hard as it took to reach her goal. She had dreamed of being in shows since her parents took her to see the film Hairspray when she was about five years old.

"Actually," Oliver said, a thoughtful look on his face, "I play the piano for a local amateur drama group, The Mixed Bunch. They are looking for a Maria for the Sound of Music. I think you would be perfect for it…." Before he could ask Maya if she would like to audition, she was out of her seat, almost jumping with excitement. Oliver laughed and handed her a leaflet with details of the group on it. "Here, take this," he said, writing a phone number on the back of the leaflet. "Call Sam and ask him to audition you. Tell him I sent you."

Maya flung her arms around Oliver's neck. "I will. Thank you so much," she said, giving him a kiss on the cheek. Oliver flushed red, which she found adorable.

"Ok, let's work on your scales." Oliver said, curbing Maya's excitement and getting the lesson back on track. The hour flew past. Maya enjoyed every minute of it. When Maya got home, she was buzzing with everything she had learned. She took out the leaflet Oliver had given her and called the number on the back. Sam was keen to meet her, so she made a date to audition for him the following day.

The following week Maya once again arrived early for her singing lesson. She let herself in the house and waited in the living room as she had before. She couldn't hear anyone in the music room but there were muffled voices coming from upstairs. A couple of minutes later Oliver came down, carrying a tray with bowl of soup that was still almost full. As he passed the living room door, he called for Maya to follow him to the kitchen where he put on the kettle for tea. "Do you want a hot drink?" He asked her, as he reached three cups down from the cupboard. Maya said she would like a tea. Oliver nodded and put teabags into each cup. "Jane, my wife, is not too well. I just need to take this up to her before we start." Maya took hers and Oliver's drinks into the lounge and started her warm-up exercises while she waited for him to come back down.

"I hear your audition went well," said Oliver, as he entered the room. Maya was stood next to the piano. She moved over to make room for him to sit down. "I think it did," replied Maya. "Sam said I would find out this week how I got on."

"Well, I have been told to start working on your solos with you. So, I guess you did very well indeed," Oliver smiled. "Congratulations. You are going to be Maria."

"Oh my god," screamed Maya, jumping up and wrapping her arms around Oliver's neck. "That's fucking amazing. I can't believe it." She let go of Oliver and pulled her phone out of her pocket. "I have to text Mum, and Alice, they will be so pleased for me. Wow, I can't believe it," she continued, shaking her head, and jiggling her foot impatiently while waiting for her mum to pick up the phone.

Maya and Oliver practiced Maria's songs from The Sound of Music. She was delighted at how much fuller and richer her voice sounded already. Oliver once again gave her some more exercises to take home, which she practiced diligently, taking it very seriously.

Three weeks in, Maya's voice had improved beyond recognition. She was blown away by how much she had achieved and was keen to start attending auditions. Her visits with Oliver were the highlight of the week. She was his last lesson of the day, so they often over ran their time and carried on talking and singing for upwards of an hour each time. Oliver was a good listener and seemed to never tire of listening to Maya talk and sing. They soon got into the habit of having a cup of tea after the lesson and moving into the lounge to chat. The conversation was usually focussed on Maya, and her hopes and dreams for the future. She enjoyed being the centre of attention and lapped up all the praise she got from Oliver.

It was late January and a thick snow had fallen. Maya was surprised to see no other footprints on the pathway as she trudged up toward Oliver's front door. Lights were on in the lounge at the front of the house, and the bedroom upstairs, but she couldn't see anyone inside from where she was standing. She turned the handle and pushed on the heavy front door to let herself in as she usually would, but the door was locked. This had never happened before, so Maya wasn't sure what to do. She checked her phone to make sure she hadn't missed a call from Oliver saying the lesson was cancelled. There were no messages, so she reached up and rang the doorbell. She heard a bit of shuffling inside and the sound of footsteps coming down the creaky wooden staircase. Oliver opened the door wearing pyjama trousers and a dressing gown. He had not shaved for what looked like a couple of days and his red rimmed eyes gave away the fact that he had recently been crying.

"I can come back another time," said Maya. She was already turning to walk away when Oliver reached out and grabbed her arm to stop her. "No, please stay," he said. "I was just about to order pizza." Maya looked him up and down, trying to assess his mood. She didn't want to stay if she was going to be intruding on anything, but on the other hand, she had grown very fond of Oliver over the past few months and wanted to be there for him if he was going through something. Finally, she agreed to stay. She was hungry, and she didn't have anywhere else to be right now, so pizza would be good. She followed Oliver into the kitchen and sat down at the counter while he rummaged around in drawers looking for his mobile phone. Maya glanced around the room, noticing that there were still breakfast dishes out on the side from this morning, and several cups and glasses were strewn across the counter haphazardly. Maya didn't know Jane well, but she knew that she would not have left a mess like that laying around if she could help it.

Oliver placed an order for food on his phone without asking Maya what she wanted. They had done this often enough now that they knew what each other would order. "Are you not ordering for Jane tonight?" Maya asked as Oliver completed the order and put his phone up on the shelf. "She is not feeling up to eating today," he responded. Maya wanted to ask him what was wrong, but she knew that was the wrong tactic with Oliver. She had to wait it out and let him speak to her about it in his own time. Asking questions would cause him to clam up. She busied herself with laying the table and getting ketchup out of the fridge. She poured herself a large glass of water and sat down to wait for the food. She had barely been seated for five minutes, when Oliver started talking. She didn't turn her head to face him, scared that if she looked at him or disturbed him in any way he would be spooked and would clam up.

When he started talking it was barely above a whisper, and Maya had to lean in close to be able to make out what he was saying. She caught the words 'returned' and 'cancer' and made a deduction from there that Jane had received the results of her biopsy that day. She scooched a little closer to Oliver on the sofa and put her arm around him to comfort him. He was stiff as a board at first, but she pulled him close, and he began sobbing. "I thought we had our whole lives. Six years we have been married. Six short years. And that is all going to be taken away from us." Oliver slid off the sofa and sat on the floor with his head in his hands. Without saying a word Maya joined him on the floor. He rested his head on her shoulder. She let him cry silently for a few minutes, stroking his hair. He was crying in earnest now, so Maya broke away and fetched a tissue and a glass of water for him before resuming her position at his side. He wiped his eyes and took a few deep breaths, seeming to gain control of himself. "Thank you, Maya. I don't know how you do it, but you always know the right thing to do to cheer me up or encourage me." He laughed gently as he wiped a tear away from his chin. "I'm supposed to be the one encouraging you." Maya brushed the comment away. "No problem. That's what friends are for. We are friends, aren't we?" she asked, looking him in the eye. Oliver held her gaze and replied. "You are more than a friend to me…"

The pizza delivery man rang the doorbell and waited patiently while both Maya and Oliver fished around in bags and on shelves to find enough change to give him a tip and have him leave. Whatever moment was about to pass between the two of them had been squashed. What did she want from him anyway? He had been about to kiss her, but was she going to kiss him back? She couldn't quite say. She liked to think she would have said no, considering he had a sick wife lying in bed mere metres above their heads, but she was not sure that she had to will-power to pull away from him. Thank goodness they had been interrupted. She would have to be more careful in future.

CHAPTER 7
MAGGIE 2019

Maggie watched as the taxi pulled away, then closed the curtains. She surveyed the room. Obviously, Alice had been too busy that evening to clear up. Maggie picked up the toys that were lying around on the floor and threw them into the open toybox. She then gathered up the cups and bowls that were strewn around the room, carried them through to the kitchen and put them into the dishwasher before flicking on the kettle and making herself a cup of coffee. She sat herself down on the couch in the kids play area and flicked through the tv channels for a while. Twenty minutes later, having found nothing to watch, Maggie wandered upstairs to check on the children. There were lots of framed, family photos on the walls all the way up. Maggie noted that most of them were quite formal, professional photos that charted the entire history of Alice and Ben's relationship. She was struck by a photo of the couple that she assumed had been their official engagement photo. The two of them looked a lot younger. There was quite an age gap, and Alice looked to be only about twenty or so. Both were smiling in the picture, and Alice was looking down at her hand and the large solitaire diamond ring she was wearing. Ben was looking at Alice and had one hand on the side of her face. They looked content and comfortable with each other. Next to that was a huge printed canvas of them two of them on their wedding day. Alice wore a beautiful wedding dress with a full veil which was spread around her face like a glowing halo in the evening sun. Ben dressed in tails, complete with top hat looked more handsome than ever. The landing at the top of the stairs was dominated by a gorgeous, hand embroidered picture of a country landscape with animals and wildflowers. Maggie took a closer look, running her hand over the fabric. Alice's name was signed in gold thread in the bottom right hand corner. The wall on the top landing was dedicated to baby photos. Maggie noticed that there were at least twenty photos of Lottie on display, but she could see none of Alfie. She wondered about that for a few minutes, coming to the conclusion that he was only six months old, and Ben and Alice were clearly a busy couple, so they probably had just not had time to arrange any photo shoots yet.

She popped her head round the door to Lottie's room. The little girl had fallen asleep diagonally across the bed and was in danger of tumbling out. Maggie scooped her up and arranged back in the bed, tucking the top sheet in at the side to make sure she didn't fall out. She was a gorgeous looking child. She had clearly received the best genes from both of her parents. Alfie was still sleeping in his parents' room. He had a cot in the corner of the room beneath another beautiful, embroidered artwork. Maggie leant over to put his dummy within reach and stroked his soft, golden hair. He groaned a little in his sleep, so Maggie backed away and perched on the end of the bed to wait for him to nod off again and not risk waking him completely. As she glanced idly round the room her eye was caught by a box on the top shelf of the open wardrobe labelled Photos. Quietly, so as not to wake Alfie, she crept across the room to take a closer look. The label on the outside of the box gave a little more detail. Family and friends 2016-17. She shook her head and turned away from the box. She wanted to look at it, but she knew that was crossing a line, so she forced herself to turn around and leave the room. Ten minutes later, she was still standing on the threshold wondering what to do.

"What harm can it be to have a quick peek.? No.one needs to know." Maggie realised she was whispering aloud to herself. It was something she did in moments of stress. She lifted the dusty box down from the shelf and sat on the bed with it. She opened the box and was dismayed to find hundreds of loose photos strewn around the box in no order whatsoever. Most had no names or dates on them. Maggie started to comb through them randomly but soon gave that up as a bad idea. There were far too many pictures in the box to do it that way. She picked up the whole box and upended it onto the king-size bed, then proceeded to sort the pictures into categories. A few minutes passed this was before she stumbled across something she had been looking for. There was a picture of Alice with Maya. Both were wearing bikinis and were posing on a beach that appeared to be on a holiday resort somewhere in Spain or Greece. Both girls were slim, blond, and tanned and were sipping on brightly coloured cocktails. She guessed the picture was about five years old as both Alice and Maya looked similar to the way they looked now. Maggie guessed that Ben was probably the one taking the picture.

Maya had a soft smile on her face, her eyes sparkling in the light from the candles on the table. She looked ethereal, like an angel. Innocent and fragile. Maggie slipped the photo into the pocket of her cardigan and returned all the other pictures to the box in such a way that she hoped neither Ben nor Alice would notice they had been touched at all. After replacing the box on the shelf, Maggie set off to explore elsewhere in the house. The spare room was set up as an office. There was a laptop, plugged into a huge monitor on a desk in the corner, with a day bed made up against the opposite wall. The day bed had been recently slept in. Maggie wondered if the Moretti's had recently had a friend to stay, or if one of them had been taking advantage of some peace and quiet away from the baby. She didn't blame them. Babies were noisy sleepers. She believed you could never get a truly good night's sleep with a baby in the room, as you would always have one ear open for a problem.

She sat herself down in the plush leather chair and swung herself around lazily for a couple of minutes until she spotted a scrapbook tucked away on one of the bookshelves. She was delighted to find it crammed full of photos of Alice and Lottie from her birth up until about she was around two years old. Maya and her son were with them in many of the photos, playing with Lottie on the swings, at the beach, feeding the ducks and at a birthday party. There were no pictures of Alice pregnant, so Maggie assumed she had stopped taking the pictures or scrapbooking them about a year ago. She wondered why that was. She flipped back to the last pages that featured Maya and Freddie. She could see that the little boy was clearly quite ill by then. His face was puffy and white while the rest of his body was painfully thin. He was small for his age, but standing next to Lottie, who was only a couple of months older than him, he looked tiny and frail. Maggie couldn't take any of those pictures without them being missed, so she contented herself with taking snaps of them on her phone.

Glancing at the time on the computer screen reminded Maggie that it was getting late. She didn't know how long Ben and Alice were going to be, so she replaced the scrap book carefully on the shelf and headed back downstairs where she grabbed her Kindle out of her handbag and settled down on the couch to read. Maggie must have dozed off, as the next thing she was aware of was the sounds of giggling outside as someone scrabbled around trying to get the key into the door lock. She stood up and folded the blanket she had wrapped around herself and laid it across the back of the sofa. Clearly Ben and Alice were in no state to be able to open the door, so she went over to open it for them. They were both clearly drunk and were leaning against each other. Maggie couldn't tell who was holding who up. "Come on in guys. I'll put the kettle on. Looks like a cup of coffee would be a good idea."

Maggie was joined in the kitchen by Ben. They could hear Alice singing along to Taylor Swift videos on YouTube. "Alice seems to have had fun" said Maggie, flicking the switch on the kettle. Ben laughed in agreement and passed her three cups from the cupboard. "Oh, I won't have one, thanks Ben, if I drink coffee now, I will be up all night"

"That sounds good to me" said Ben with a lascivious grin. Unsure if she had heard him correctly Maggie turned to face him. He was looking at her chest in a way that made her instantly uncomfortable. She turned her back on him to fill the cups and he stepped up behind her and circled her waist in a tight hug. Attempting to distract him with humour Maggie said "I wouldn't do that while I have a kettle in my hand" She attempted to shake him free, but he was holding her tightly, his hands started to wander down over her thighs. With some force she pushed him back and grabbed the two cups to hold out as a barrier between them. "I have to go" She said. "Alice will be waiting for her drink" She left the room and he followed a few footsteps behind her. Alice was sitting on the couch looking a little the worse for wear. The alcohol was clearly starting to show its effects. Maggie handed her the coffee and encouraged her to drink up. Alice was definitely going to suffer in the morning. Ben took a seat next to Alice and taking the TV controls he started to flip through the channels. He acted as if neither of the women were there, which was fine by Maggie. The longer she spent in his company, the more repulsive she found him. She wondered how often he found himself rubbing up against other women and felt sorry for her new friend. Maggie said her goodbyes as soon as she could.

CHAPTER 8
MAYA 2019

Not too long-ago Maya would have walked down the side alley and let herself in the back door of Alice's house. She couldn't remember why or how that had changed. She thought about their friendship as she waited for Alice to open the front door. They had known each other for years and had been close before the children were born. She was godmother to both Lottie and Alfie. Alice had been a rock when Maya had fallen pregnant with Freddie. Looking back Maya wondered how she would have coped as a young mother without the support of her friend. Her parents had been less than pleased when she had dropped out of school to have her baby. She was in her first year at drama college, and everything was going so well for her. It was all she had ever wanted to do. She had a minor role in a west end play lined up, but three days into rehearsals she had started to throw up in the mornings. Within a couple of weeks, the morning sickness was so bad that she was unable to leave the house before mid-morning. She had started skipping morning sessions and turning up around lunchtime once her stomach had settled down. She had managed like that for about a month before the director had called her in for a meeting and told her she was being replaced. Very soon after that she had a similar meeting with the head of the college. Maya had withdrawn from the college there and then. Alice was her only friend throughout that time, which Maya now recognised as among the lowest of her life. She had asked who the father was, but when Maya refused to say, she had respected her friends wishes and had never asked again. With

Alice's help, Maya had planned for the future. She had helped her find a flat and had arranged benefits to help her raise her child. As expected, her parents had been upset. Her mum had shouted and cried, disappointed that Maya had ruined her life.

Despite her concerns, Maya had never seen things that way. Freddie had not ruined her life. It was true she would never be a singer now and would never be starring in the west end, but she had replaced that dream with the dream of a stable life for her little boy. Alice had been with her through the whole thing. Even though she was going through her own pregnancy and birth. They had attended childbirth classes together and Alice had held Maya's hair while she threw up. When Ben had been held up at work and not made it to Lottie's birth, Maya had been there as Alice's birth partner. She had cut the cord when her god-daughter had come into the world and shared the magical first hour with Alice and Lottie before Ben turned up to relieve her. Three months later, when it was her turn to give birth, Alice had been with Maya throughout the whole thing. Eighteen hours of labour followed by a traumatic caesarean had not phased Alice one bit. She had held hands with her friend from start to finish without a single complaint. For the first six months of Freddie's life, she and Alice had seen each other every day. They went shopping, visited the health centre and walked in the park together. Maya ate with Alice and Ben at least four times a week and often stayed overnight in their spare room snuggled on the single bed with Freddie.

Thinking about it, Maya realised that it was once Freddie had started to get ill that there had been a subtle shift in their relationship. Alice was still her best friend, but Ben had started to make comments about her being down all the time. It was obvious he cared about her and her son, but Maya couldn't help but notice that he would subtly shut her down when she started to talk about anything that he considered negative. He wouldn't tolerate talk about Freddie's hospital appointments and treatments. Eventually she stopped even mentioning them. The visits to the house slowed, and eventually stopped altogether, without anything ever being said by any of them. If Alice was upset that Maya didn't visit anymore, she never mentioned it or asked why. The two women still spoke whenever they met and were in contact via text most days, but the sisterly bond they had shared had been stretched beyond recognition. Maya had been so caught up with looking after Freddie and balancing her life to suit his appointments that she had never had time to miss the relationship with her best friend. She had barely had time to think about herself recently but standing here on the doorstep she had a sudden feeling of overwhelming loss. She realised with shocking intensity the depth of her loneliness over the past two and a half years.

By the time Alice answered the door, Maya's tears were in full flow. Alice took one look at her friend and stepped forward to take her in her arms for a long, hug. "I've missed you," whispered Alice into the mass of curls in the taller woman's hair. Maya let out a sob. "I've missed you too." They stood that way for a few seconds on the doorstep before Alice broke the embrace and guided Maya into the house. Lottie spotted her immediately she entered and run up to her, flinging her arms around her with glee, clearly delighted to see her 'Aunty' again after all this time. If Maya had thought it was going to be awkward, she was wrong. The two women seemed to get on with their friendship at if nothing had ever happened, starting again where they had left off, almost three years ago.

It was Saturday afternoon. Ben was still at work and Alice had been sitting on the couch watching cartoons with the children and nursing a substantial hangover when Maya had knocked on the door. She had felt instantly better for seeing her old friend. Once Maya had managed to extricate herself from Lottie, and a new film had been loaded into the DVD player, the two women moved to the kitchen table to continue their conversation.

Alice asked after Freddie. Maya explained he was spending the day with her parents and went on to explain about the donation. "So, someone has put forward all the money for the fundraiser. The whole amount. Can you believe it?" She was practically glowing with happiness. "Think of what this will mean for the hospital. We will be able to kit out the whole play area now. And provide beds for the parent's room," Alice smiled, delighted to see her friend looking so happy. She had not seen her like this for years now. "So, who made the donation? Do you know them?" asked Alice. Maya shrugged and shook her head. "I can't remember the name off the top of my head, but its no-one I know. Just a random stranger. Someone doing a good deed. How awesome is that?" She finished, with a broad grin. "Hey, where's Ben?" continued Maya, looking around the room.

Alice heard the key turn in the front door. "Sounds like he is here now," she smiled. Maya and Ben had always got on like a house on fire. Maya jumped up to face the door, half running to meet Ben as he entered. The two embraced and Alice smiled as Maya recounted everything that she had told her about the mystery donation to Ben. He seemed as happy as they were with the news. "How is Freddie?" asked Ben. "People ask me about him all the time." Freddie was something of a celebrity locally. Everyone in the town knew who he was and had followed his journey back to health as closely as if he was their own family.

Alice told Maya she needed to feed the children and get them ready for bed. Maya offered to help as she had some free time, but Alice would have none of it. "It's ok, why don't you have a glass of wine and catch up with Ben and when I'm done, we can get a takeaway or something?" Maya thought about it for a second, wondering if she should check on Freddie. No, he would be fine. He loved spending time with his grandparents, and they were right, she did need some time to be herself now that he was better. "That sounds lovely," she said, as Ben handed her a glass of red wine.

Three hours and three bottles of wine later, the pizza had all been eaten and the three of them were all tipsy. Maya had called her parents who had told her not to worry about Freddie as they were going to keep him overnight. Alice was the first to tire. "I'm sorry both of you, but I am gonna have to call it a night." Her words were a little slurred, and Maya had to admit that she did look very tired. "I can't handle two late nights in a row anymore." Ben laughed, aiming for good natured, but coming off snarky. "It's hardly a late night. Its 9pm. In the past we would just be getting ready to go out now." Alice shook her head and forced herself up of the couch. "Nope. I need my bed." She staggered over and gave Maya a hug. "Thank you for a lovely evening. I'm so glad about the money. Call me in the morning." Maya kissed her on the forehead. "Night Alice. Love you." Alice blew her a kiss and the two of them listened and laughed as she bounced off the walls on the way up to her bedroom.

"More wine?" asked Ben. It was more a statement than a question as he was already topping up her glass again. Maya kicked off her shoes and tucked her feet up on the sofa under Ben, laying her head down on the armrest. "Was it you?" she asked. "Did you give the donation?" She looked at Ben, who had rearranged himself on the sofa next to her. "What makes you think that?" he replied. Maya thought about it for a moment, noticing that he didn't deny it. "I know you have always looked out for me and Freddie. It seems like something you would do." Ben leaned over and pulled her to him, putting his arm around her shoulder and kissing her on the forehead. "I love you both. You deserve to be happy. I think we have a bottle of tequila. Let's celebrate." Ben jumped up, making Maya laugh as she half fell off the sofa with his sudden movement. "Yay tequila!" she giggled, holding out her hand to Ben to pull her up from where she sat. The two of them spent a happy hour doing shots and catching up, sharing funny stories about their children until almost Midnight, when Maya called a taxi.

"I've had a great night," said Maya as Ben helped her on with her coat at the door. "I've missed you. Let's not wait so long next time." Ben put his arms around her and hugged her good-bye. "I've missed you too. Give Freddie a big kiss from me." She agreed she would and gave his hand a squeeze as she walked carefully down the drive to the waiting taxi and blew him a kiss as she closed the door. Ben was still watching her from the door as the taxi turned the corner.

CHAPTER 9
ALICE 2015

Smallhaven was, by definition, a small town, so a pretty, blonde stranger in a bright red coat was bound to draw attention. Alice had been searching the windows of the estate agency for some 8-10 minutes before becoming aware of the handsome, olive skinned man inside the shop. He was openly staring at her and when he caught her eye his face broke into a beaming grin. Flustered at having been observed she smiled back and straightened her coat before entering the shop. The man stood as she entered and thrust out his hand in greeting. "Hi, I'm Ben, Ben Moretti. How can I help?" Alice shook his hand and sat down, smoothing her coat over her lap. "Hi Ben" She said, returning his smile. "I'm new to town. I'm looking for a flat. One bedroom, not too scummy. Got anything like that? The ones in the window are beautiful, but a little over my price range sadly." Ben riffled through the large, messy pile of paperwork on his desk. "Yes, I do. There are a couple of places that are just about to come on the market. I looked them over last week. Not too far from the train station and on a bus route, so perfect for the university. I can take you there now if you like?" He handed her the details. "How did you know I am going to Uni?" she asked, intrigued. "He winked at her. "I know things. I could sense it"

"Really? Do I look that much like a student?"

"No, not really. I just noticed the prospectus sticking out the top of your bag and took a wild guess. Doesn't always work out but makes me look clever when it does." Alice laughed and looked over the details for a couple of minutes. Ben watched her as she read. She held her head to one side, the hair brushed behind her ear, and he could see her biting her lip slightly in concentration. "Ok" she said, "let's start with this one." She pointed at a Victorian house that had been split into two separate flats. It overlooked a park, near the beach. Ben jumped up and almost ran around the table to pull the chair out for her. Alice couldn't help but be flattered by his obvious attraction to her. She waited at the door while Ben grabbed his coat and the keys to the pool car that sat out the front of the shop. "It's not far from here," he said. He opened the car door for her, and Alice slid into the passenger seat. Ben took the opportunity on the journey to give Alice a running commentary about the town. He seemed to know an awful lot about the local history of the place and clearly loved the town. Several people waved at him as he drove past, and Ben shared titbits of information about all of them. Alice found it endearing how much he obviously cared about where he lived and the people he shared the town with.

They arrived at the first flat within ten minutes or so. Alice knew immediately that she would take it. The house was built of flint, with a red wooden front door and wisteria growing up the walls. She loved it and hoped that the inside would not disappoint. Ben fished the keys out of his pocket and opened up, leading the way up the stairs. The door opened on to a decent sized living room with a view out over the beach green and the sea beyond. The full height windows let in loads of light. Alice could imagine setting up her easel next to the window and working there. The bedroom didn't disappoint, having the same aspect as the lounge, with the bathroom and compact kitchen at the back of the building. "No need to see more," said Alice with a smile, "when can I move in?" Ben raised his eyebrows.

"Ok then. That was easy. I didn't even have to give you the hard sell," he laughed. "Let's head back and sort out the paperwork then I guess." Alice detected a note of disappointment. "I thought you would be happy. I mean, don't you get commissions or something?"

"Well, yes," said Ben, "But I was hoping to have you in the car for a little bit longer so I could work up the courage to ask you out." He looked at her sideways and she returned his smile. "I'm not looking for a date right now. Thank you for asking though."

She felt bad that she had turned him down, but she was determined to give her all at university and didn't need the distraction of a boyfriend. Her parents had both died in a car crash when she was just nine years old, and she had lived with her aunt Emma ever since. Emma had tried her best to look after Alice, but she was not cut out to be a Mother. They had a more of a sisterly type of friendship. She had a brother, Shane, who was twelve years older than her, but she had lost touch with him some years ago. He lived in New Zealand somewhere with his boyfriend and their two cats. Their parents had left both children a small chunk of money, enough for Alice to buy a small flat and pay her way through the three years of University if she was sensible. Ben looked deflated. He started the car and pulled out into the traffic in silence. Alice felt obliged to explain. "Hey Ben, this has nothing to do with you. You are lovely, and usually I would jump at the chance of a date with you," she began, "But my degree is going to be intense and will take up a lot of my time. It wouldn't be fair to you." She turned to look at him to see how he was reacting to what she was saying. He was nodding, and although he still didn't look entirely happy, she was pleased enough to see how interested he was in her plans. "I have a plan you see. Eventually I am going to own a boutique selling fabrics and outfits I have designed. It's my dream." She smiled and looked wistfully out of the car window, lost in her thoughts.

On the way back to the shop, Ben asked Alice if he could see some of her designs someday. She suspected it was just another ploy to get her to go on a date with him. ", I have a friend who does a bit of fashion design. I thought she might like to see some of your work. She is always saying she needs to find someone fresh and young to work with. Just thought it would help" Alice spun round in the chair to see him better.

"Really? Oh, that would be so great. I have my portfolio at the hotel. That's so kind of you" Ben smiled at her excitement.

"That surely must be worth a date?" he grinned.

"Let's see if she likes my work first" Alice pushed him playfully on the arm. "I'm staying at the Travelodge on Raven Road until the flat is sorted out. My portfolio is there. You can text me when you have spoken to your friend if you like." She scribbled her number on a post-it from her bag and stuck it on to the dash in front of her, before sitting back up in her seat. "I think I'm going to like it here." Ben glanced at her in the side mirror. She looked happy.

CHAPTER 10
ALICE 2019

Alice opened the bathroom cabinet, making sure to avoid looking at herself in the mirror. She had a pounding headache surging behind her eyes. She had to have some painkillers somewhere. She pulled out all the boxes and bottles, barely noticing them bouncing off the basin onto the floor. Where were the goddamn pills? With a sigh she pulled the dressing gown belt tight around her waist and headed down to the entrance hall to find her handbag. Maybe there were a couple of rogue pills hiding in there. As she walked down the stairs, careful to hold on to the rail in case a bout of nausea and vertigo sent her tumbling down, she could hear the children in the kitchen. She had left Alfie strapped in his highchair while Lottie played with play doh on the table next to him. She wished they would just fall asleep or be quiet for a while. She couldn't remember the last time she had had a full night's sleep. Alfie was still waking every hour in the night. She hated to leave him crying. Every whimper made her worry that there was something wrong with him. Even if she had been inclined to subscribe to the controlled crying technique, she never would have been able to do it. Ben needed his sleep. He had a high-pressured job, and now he was running for mayor he was busier than ever. It was only fair she supposed that she do all the night-time feeds and nappy changes. Digging around in the bottom of the bag she found a lone paracetamol, out of its packet and covered in lint. That would have to do. She took her prize into the kitchen to find a glass of water. As she walked in both children immediately started clamouring for her attention. She turned her back on them and filled her glass from the cold tap, swallowing the pill down quickly. "Please be quiet" she whispered to herself. "please be quiet, please be quiet. Be quiet" she spun round, stunned to find that she had screamed the last two words into the shocked faces of her two children and that she still had the glass in her hand raised above her head as if she was about to strike them with it. She collapsed down onto the kitchen chair, sobbing, gathering both children into her arms, her tears and wails mingling with theirs.

There was a knock on the front door, followed by the sound of someone calling her name. Alice contemplated for a minute just ignoring the caller, but she knew the three of them had just been making enough noise that half the neighbourhood would have heard them, and her car was parked out front on the drive way. She hastily returned the children to their seats, throwing crisps into a bowl for them and splashing water on her face. "Coming" she called as she did her best to smooth her hair down with her hands and adjust the dressing gown to cover the stains of last night's dinner on her pyjamas. She peered through the little window in the middle of the door to see Maggie standing there holding a bunch of flowers and a large white cake box. Alice took a calming breath and plastered her best fake smile onto her face before opening the door and beckoning Maggie in.

To Maggie's credit she managed not to make it obvious that she was surprised by Alice's appearance. Taking the lead Maggie steered her toward the kitchen and indicated for her to take a seat while she busied herself making tea. She kept up a constant stream of chatter as she bustled around putting dirty dinner plates into the dishwasher and wiping over the surfaces. When the kettle boiled, she took the drinks and joined Alice at the table. Alice knew Maggie was worried about her. She should probably put on a brave face and sort herself out, but she just felt exhausted. She had never felt so tired in her life. She didn't even have the energy to talk. Maggie was asking her a question. She realised that she had been talking to her for the past five minutes, but she had not heard a word. She forced herself to look Maggie in the face, but when she saw the concern and worry in her eyes it was all too much and Alice sank down onto the table in despair. She sobbed. Her shoulders shaking with the force of the emotion. She felt Maggie put a reassuring hand on her back, which simply caused her to cry even more. She had felt so alone for so long that this simple gesture pushed her over the edge. She was vaguely aware of Maggie leaving to deal with the children. Alfie was crying somewhere behind her, but she just couldn't bring herself to care. When she thought about the children she was overcome by a feeling of resentment, bordering on hatred. If she hadn't had the children, she would be free. She could go anywhere. She wouldn't be stuck in this house in an endless monotonous cycle of cleaning, cooking, and shopping. Instead she could be travelling the world or living on a houseboat selling her art for a living. Even thinking like this made her hate herself. What kind of mother resents her own children? Was she really that terrible a person? Maggie was urging her to drink her tea now. She dutifully obeyed, even nibbling on one of the biscuits that had appeared on the table in front of her. It had been so long since someone had done something for her, simply to cheer her up or make her happy, that she had almost forgotten what it was, or how to respond to it.

An hour later, after several more cups of tea and a shower that Maggie had insisted she take, Alice was feeling much better. She sat at the dressing table in the bedroom she shared with Ben and looked at her bruises in the broken mirror. She had had worse. Luckily, it was an overcast day, so she could wear long sleeves without arousing suspicion. She brushed her hair, slicked on some lip gloss, and headed downstairs. Both the children were napping, and Maggie was sitting in the lounge flicking through a magazine. She put the magazine down on the arm of the couch next to her and looked up at Alice "You look better. How are you feeling?" Alice was embarrassed that Maggie had seen her in such a state, but she knew there was no point trying to hide anything. Maggie had cleaned up the mess in the living room from the argument she had had with Ben the previous night, so there was no fooling her.

"It was just a silly argument," Alice began. "It was my fault. I said some things I shouldn't have, and it got out of hand. It was nothing really." Maggie didn't look convinced. "He loves me. He really does….and the kids," Alice continued, though she didn't know if she was saying that for Maggie's benefit or her own. "He's under a lot of pressure at the moment" Maggie leant across to take Alice's hand. "You don't need to say anything," she began. "I'm here if you need me ok?" Alice nodded. ", I had something I would like to ask you," said Maggie, changing the subject to try to put Alice at ease. "I saw your beautiful wall hangings upstairs. I wondered if I could commission you to make some for me to hang in my lounge? I think they would look perfect there." Alice was flattered. She had not done any embroidery or artwork since before Lottie was born. Just the thought of it cheered her up. Immediately ideas and designs started swirling around in her mind. "I would love to. I have some pictures of my other designs on my phone I can show you." Alice said, looking around for her mobile. Maggie pulled a mobile phone with a shattered screen from her pocket and handed it to Alice. "I found this on the floor. Sorry. We could try taking it to the phone shop in town if you are up for a walk?" She suggested. Alice thought it would do her good to get some fresh air, so when the children woke the two women strapped them in the buggy and set off.

It was a beautiful day and although they were almost a mile away from the sea Alice could smell the sea air on the breeze. The sun was hot on her face and she had a sudden urge to confide in Maggie. Alice didn't have many friends as Ben and the children took up all her time. She had been touched by Maggie trying to help her at home, and although she knew there was nothing that Maggie could do to help her, it would be nice just to speak to another woman. The only friend she had was Maya, and she was not exactly the type of person you would share your innermost feelings with.

"Ben didn't break the phone" She said, looking at Maggie to get her reaction. "He accused me of cheating on him. As if!" She snorted. "I'm too tired to do anything with him right now, let alone find someone new. Anyway, it seems that he took it upon himself to get a nanny-cam if you can believe that." Maggie kept her face neutral, which encouraged Alice to continue. She couldn't bear to feel that people were judging her. She liked that Maggie didn't comment and was content to hear her out. "So, yesterday he accused me of flirting with the supermarket delivery guy. I told him he was imagining it, but he said he had heard me tell him he had big muscles or something. Well, I remember saying to the guy that he didn't need to go to the gym as he was lifting heavy bags all day, and I was about to defend myself, when I realised that he had no way of knowing that. That's when he showed me the footage on his phone. He had a recording of me taking the Tesco delivery. Apparently, there is a camera in the light fitting in the hallway."

Maggie looked concerned; her eyebrows drawn together in a worried frown. "My god Alice. What did you say to that?" Alice winced. "I threw his phone at him. That's how it got smashed"

She sighed, letting her shoulders drop "I shouldn't have done it. It just made him angrier. We ended up having a blazing row and he stormed out. When he didn't come home by 2am, I locked all the doors and went to bed," she sighed, feeling down once again. "I know it's wrong and I was angry at first, but he only gets jealous because he loves me." Maggie stopped walking and turning to face Alice she took both of her hands and looked her in the eye. "People in love don't hurt their partners or secretly film them. You deserve to be trusted." Alice pulled away. Disappointed that Maggie didn't get it after all. Ben was a good person, he had his faults, but most of them could be traced back to his childhood. He shouldn't be punished forever because bad things happened to him when he was young. "I know he didn't mean it," said Alice. "It was all a misunderstanding. I shouldn't have overreacted. I'm so dumb." Maggie shook her head. "You are not dumb, Alice, or stupid or ugly or untrustworthy or any of the other things he has made you feel about yourself. You deserve to be loved and trusted. You've done nothing wrong."

The two women had walked through town to the local park. Both children were sleeping in the buggy, so Alice steered them toward a park bench and sat down, turning her face to the sun, and closing her eyes to soak in the autumn rays. With her eyes still firmly closed, Alice continued "I never used to be this useless. I was a confident person once. I don't know when I became this person." Maggie sat down next to her and put an arm around her shoulder for Alice to rest her head. "All my self-confidence started slipping away once I got pregnant. I think that was what changed everything. I don't think I've been happy since then" Saying the words out loud were enough to push Alice over the edge again. She burst into tears once more, unable to continue with her story. She had fully intended to tell Maggie everything, but just couldn't bring herself to when crunch time came. She just wasn't ready to open that particular can of worms yet.

CHAPTER 11
MAYA 2015

Maya ran from the bus all the way to Oliver's house, clutching her letter tightly. She could barely contain her excitement as she gave a quick knock on the door and barged into the house to find him. She had nailed the audition that afternoon and been given an unconditional offer to study drama at her first choice of college. Not only that, but there had been agents in the audience who had already approached her about auditioning for roles in the West End. Everything they had been working for over the past months had come good and Maya couldn't wait to see Oliver's face when she told him about it. He had offered to come with her to the audition, but she had turned him down. She thought she would be too nervous if anyone she knew was watching. She hadn't let her mum come either. She hadn't even let her mum drive her there. The two of them had fallen out about it that morning, but Maya knew this news would more than make up for her disappointment. She had already called her mum to give her the good news, but she thought Oliver deserved to hear it from her directly as he had done so much to help her get there.

It was late afternoon and the sun was setting, plunging the house into shadow. Maya didn't even bother to turn on the lights as she almost ran to the lounge to find Oliver. She pushed open the heavy internal door and jumped as a loud pop and a stream of confetti and paper streamers fluttered around her head. Her hands flew to her mouth and she half laughed half screamed as the adrenaline pumped through her. Oliver was standing in front of a big Congratulations sign, holding a smoking party popper with a hopeful look on his face. Maya couldn't quite catch her breath to say anything, so she made do with nodding. Oliver scooped her into his arms and swung her around " I knew you could do it" he said as he set her gently back on her feet and reached for the bottle of champagne he had on ice on the coffee table. Maya giggled as she took a seat on the sofa. "It's a good job I did, cos you would look a proper tit right now if I had failed".

"You have such a way with words" Oliver laughed, as he poured her a large glass of champagne and clinked glasses with her. He congratulated her again and took a huge swig. Maya did the same, enjoying the way the bubbles fizzed in the back of her nose. She was not much of a drinker, having only ever drunk before at a couple of parties. She started to feel a little giddy in a way that was not at all unpleasant. Oliver landed heavily on the sofa next to her. She could vaguely smell some stronger alcohol on his breath. Maybe Whiskey. He had obviously started her celebration drinks without her. "So" he said "tell me all about it. What was it like?" He was watching her intently, with a slightly glazed look in his eyes. Maya couldn't tell if he had been crying again, or if the whisky was just taking its toll. She drained her glass of champagne and topped it back up, before recounting the entire day in detail. Oliver listened to every word, without taking his eyes off her. Maya was mesmerized by his gaze. She couldn't tell if it was the effects of the champagne or the way he was looking at her, but Maya was totally drawn in by him. When he leaned in to kiss her, she responded with a desire she didn't know she possessed.

It was late by the time Maya awoke. The candles had burned down to nothing and the only light in the room came from the streetlights outside. She took a second to take stock of her bearings. She was lying on the floor, wrapped in a throw from the sofa with a half-naked Oliver snoring quietly beside her. She disentangled herself from the cover and felt around for her dress, throwing it over her head before fumbling for the lamp switch. Her head was spinning slightly from the champagne and she was parched. She covered Oliver again with the throw as it was starting to get chilly and headed into the kitchen for a glass of water. Her mobile vibrated in her pocket so she pulled it out to see who it was, noticing as she swiped the screen open that she had fourteen missed calls from her mum. She didn't need to listen to the voicemail to know that she would be wondering where Maya had got to, so she texted her back, and told her she had been to a party with her friends and that she would be home soon so not to worry. She then called a taxi and gathering up the rest of her things so as not to wake Oliver, she stepped out onto the pavement to wait. Her parents were asleep by the time Maya got home. It had been an eventful day and evening, and she felt as if her whole life had changed.

It was a few days before Maya had a chance to get back to see Oliver. She had put on her best underwear and made an extra effort with her make up. She arrived at the house a little early, and there was still a student in with Oliver. It was a nice day, so Maya chose to sit and wait on the wall at the front of the house and enjoy the sunshine. The student came out a few minutes later, and once he had walked away Maya jumped off the wall and headed back inside. Oliver came to the door before she could let herself in. He had a sombre expression on his face. She stood at the door in front of him, her smile fading as she realised he was not stepping aside to let her in. She reached out to touch his arm, but he pulled away. It was only a slight movement, but to her it felt like an earthquake. She knew what was coming before he even opened his mouth to speak. "Maya, I'm sorry..." he began. Maya put her hand up to cut him off and turned to walk away. "Save it Oliver. I don't want to hear it." She reached the gate, and he came running after her, grabbing her arm to slow her down. She shook him off and turned angrily to face him. "What? What do you want to say? That you are sorry that you used me to make yourself feel better? That you really didn't mean to hurt me? That you are sticking with your wife and can't see me anymore?" Oliver dropped his arm to his side and stared at her with his mouth open. "Well?" said Maya. "is that what you wanted to say?" She stared at him fiercely with her arms crossed for a couple of beats. "Yep. Thought so." Maya stormed off down the road without looking back.

CHAPTER 12
MAGGIE 2019

Maggie hadn't seen much of Alice for a few days. She was starting to think that maybe she was avoiding her, when she got a phone call out of the blue inviting her to go for a coffee. Alice had chosen an out of town soft play centre so Lottie could go entertain herself while the two of them talked. Maggie pulled into the car park a few minutes early and was pleased to see that Alice's car was already there. She was not keen on walking into somewhere like that without a child. She was aware that it could look odd. Once inside Lottie spotted her immediately and came running over to hug her legs. Maggie swung her up into her arms and gave her a hug. The noise of the place was deafening, and she had to strain to hear the little girl's chatter. When Maggie made it to the table Alice had reserved for them, she set Lottie down on the floor and watched as she skipped away to join her friends. She was glad to see that Alice was looking much better than the last time they had met. She was breastfeeding Alfie under a muslin cloth and couldn't get up, so Maggie kissed her hello then headed over to the coffee stand to buy them both a latte. By the time she got back to the table Alfie had finished eating and was starting to nod off. Alice laid him in his pushchair and rocked him with her foot.

"I forgot how noisy these places are," said Maggie as she pulled her chair in closer so they could converse without resorting to shouting. "Thanks for coming," started Alice, taking a sip from her drink. "that's good coffee. I need the caffeine today." Maggie refrained from pointing out that Alice said that every day. She had two children under four and a busy home and social life, she had every right to be tired. Maggie was keen to ask about how things were at home for Alice after the row the other night, but she couldn't think of a way to ask that didn't sound crass or nosey. Instead she thought she would try to find out a bit more about Maya. "So, do you have a lot of friends in Smallhaven?" She asked, by way of starting conversation. "Oh, not that many really" Alice replied, distractedly watching Lottie argue over a piece of play equipment. "I know a lot of people through Ben, but I only have one proper friend, Maya. Her picture was up in my house. You probably saw it. Blonde, white teeth, perfect body?" Maggie nodded, "Yes I saw it. What's her story?"

"Actually, she is much nicer in real life than you would imagine," she told Maggie. "I've known her almost as long as I have been in Smallhaven. We met at a theatre group. She was their leading lady and I was the pleb who painted the sets. We hit it off and have been friends ever since, which frankly is as much a mystery to me as it is to everyone else. She is so different to me." She put her hand on her chin and pondered for a minute. "She is much nicer to everyone when she is not working. Catch her in work mode and she is a straight up Bitch." Maggie laughed. "Anyway" Alice said, continuing her story and enjoying having someone to tell it to. "We were pregnant together. Maya had Freddie about 3 months after I had Lottie. She didn't have a boyfriend or anything, so I agreed to be her birth partner as she had done the same for me. I drove her to the hospital when she was five centimetres dilated and I was still there more than twenty-six hours later when she was at nine centimetres. I thought her labour was never going to end. At one point we joked that the baby would be old enough to start school by the time it arrived." Maggie gave a low giggle, which encouraged Alice to talk some more. "She eventually gave birth to Freddie after nearly thirty-four hours labour, she was so strong, bless her. Do you know, as soon as he was placed on her chest, Maya asked me to be his Godmother?" She grinned in delight, reliving the scene in her mind. "Of course, I said yes. Freddie was a trouper, just like his mother. I love that boy." Maggie nodded. "He is adorable," she agreed.

"It must have been nice having someone with a baby the same age to spend time with," said Maggie, encouraging Alice to keep talking.

"It was great at first. We were inseparable. Maya spent loads of time at ours at the beginning. She gets on great with Ben, and we had so much to talk about. But it all got a bit difficult when Freddie got sick. I think it was hard for her to see Lottie doing so well while Freddie was getting more and more unwell. We just sort of lost touch after that. Sad really." Alice stared distractedly at Alfie, who was contentedly sitting on her lap watching the older children playing. "Sorry, there I go talking about myself the whole time," Alice said apologetically.

Before long, talk turned to Maggie. Alice wanted to know what she was planning to do to support herself. Maggie didn't need to work. Between the inheritance from her parents and the insurance money she had more than enough to keep her going for quite some time, but she knew that if she didn't do something she would get bored. "Well, there is one idea I have been toying with" she said. "I have always had this desire to own a little, old fashioned tearoom." She looked at Alice who smiled and nodded her encouragement. "I have a memory of going on holiday with my parents when I was about 10. We were at this beautiful little tearoom in Cornwall. There were scones and jam and a huge dish of buttery clotted cream. Everything was served on an old-fashioned tea service and my mum let me pour the tea myself from the big flowery teapot using a proper tea strainer. That's one of the last memories of my family all together. They died in the car crash the next year. Ever since then I have had a dream to open a tearoom like that."

"That sounds wonderful," said Alice. "Smallhaven could use a place like that."

"That's what I have been thinking. I would love to open a little tearoom looking out over the sea or the river, selling proper tea made from tea leaves, and homemade cakes and scones. Heaven." Alice smiled at her. "I think that's a winner. There is nowhere around here like that." She was excited about it and Maggie could almost see the plans forming in her head. "I know the very place for it. Let's get out of here and I will show you. Can you grab Lottie for me? I will sort Alfie out. Have you got time for a quick detour?" Maggie agreed that she had. She was intrigued now and was pleased that Alice had not dismissed her idea or laughed at her. She had never told her dream to anyone before. Now she had said it out loud it felt as if it could be a possibility. She didn't know whether to be scared or excited.

Ten minutes later the kids were in the car with Alice, and Maggie was following them out of the car park in her little Fiat 500. She didn't know the area very well still, but she could tell they were heading toward the seafront area. Alice eventually pulled up alongside the abandoned lifeboat station, so Maggie parked up behind her and wandered over to help her unload the children. Alice jumped out of the car. "So, what do you think?" Maggie looked around unsure what Alice was expecting her to say. "What am I supposed to be looking at? I thought we were going to look at a teashop?" Alice grabbed her arm and turned her to face the old building. "We are. Look at this place. It's perfect." Maggie did as she was asked. The building was right next to the river mouth, with huge glass doors facing out toward the open sea. Maggie had to admit that the view was breath-taking, but it was far from the vision she had of a cosy little shop on a crowded high street. "I don't know Alice; it looks like a giant garage. I wouldn't even know where to start," she said, creases forming above her nose as she stared doubtfully at the building

"Well, that's ok," Alice replied "cos I do. This place could be amazing. Imagine opening those huge doors in the summer and having tables all set out here by the river. And look at the huge space inside. Once that is painted white with an enormous chandelier in the centre you will have a beautiful space. Contemporary, but elegant." She gesticulated with her arms, demonstrating where everything would go, explaining to Maggie that vision that was almost fully formed in her artist's mind already. She could see by the excited look on Maggie's face that she was starting to win her over. "It's an art deco building, so you could go full 1920s flapper girl crazy." Maggie smiled and peered through the grime on the windows. That idea did sound kind of great. She couldn't help but be infected by Alice's enthusiasm. It would certainly be unusual, and she was excited by the Art Deco theme. "We need to get in there and have a look" She said. Alice pointed to the letting agents board on the side of the building and grinned. "Luckily, I happen to know the agent."

While Alice called Ben to arrange for someone to bring the keys down for them to have a look, Maggie wandered around the area. The building sat on its own plot with a large car parking area behind it. The station consisted of a large, high ceilinged main workshop, where the lifeboat had been stored. This was where the full height glass doors were located. Attached to that there was a single storey building, which Maggie assumed was where supplies were stored and where the crew operated from. Either side of the building were flats and houses that overlooked the river. In fact, she could see her own flat from here, less than half a mile from this spot. The new lifeboat station was situated on the other side of the river about half a mile in the opposite direction. A paved boardwalk joined this area to the seafront, and Maggie was pleased to see that even though it was not a particularly warm day and there was the threat of rain in the air, there were still plenty of pedestrians and dog walkers taking their daily exercise. By the time one of Ben's employees arrived with the keys Maggie had already made up her mind that this was the place. She would make it work. She knew she could.

CHAPTER 13
ALICE 2015

Alice couldn't think who would be ringing on her door on a Saturday afternoon. She had only been living in the new flat for a week and hadn't had time to meet many people yet. Assuming it was a delivery person, she pressed the entry button on the intercom without asking who it was. Glancing through the patterned glass beside the door a minute later she was pleasantly surprised to see Ben standing on the doorstep holding an enormous pot plant. She hurriedly brushed her hair down with her hands and adjusted her clothes before opening the door. He smiled at her from behind the bushy foliage. "Hi, any chance I can put this thing down, it weighs a tonne" Alice laughed and stepped aside to let him in, following him back into the flat where he put the plant down on the coffee table. "Is this all part of the service, or are you flirting with me Ben Moretti?" Alice asked Playfully. " Well, that depends" he replied "If you are not interested in me, it's just me providing excellent customer service and a nice gift to remember me by, but if you are interested, then this is a housewarming gift and I can ask you out for dinner. It's up to you." Alice picked up the plant and carried it over to a spot on the windowsill. She could tell he was watching her and waiting for her reaction and she enjoyed stringing out the moment. "Well. Thank you for the beautiful housewarming gift. Where are we going for dinner?" Alice was amused to see that Ben let out a sigh of relief. He had obviously been holding his breath. Maybe he wasn't quite as confident as he made out to be. After a brief chat they decided to go to the little Italian restaurant in town. Alice had walked past it a couple of times and was keen to try it. Ben agreed to pick her up at 7.30 that evening, which gave her a few hours to unpack her clothes and find something decent to wear.

Alice had not had many boyfriends. She had always been a bit of a loner. She had dated a bit when she was in the 6th form, but those boys all seemed so childish compared to Ben. He was quite a bit older than her, but he had boyish good looks, so it was difficult to guess his age exactly. She thought he was probably in his mid-twenties. Every time she had seen him, he had been wearing a suit, so she thought she should probably dress up for the occasion. She settled on a long, floral maxi dress with a short pink jacket and matching sandals. She was not one for make-up usually, but she put on some lip gloss and a bit of eye shadow and mascara to bring out her eyes. She scrunch dried her hair with a bit of mousse after her shower and left it loose. Looking in the mirror she was pleased with the results. She was just cramming her purse and phone into a little beaded clutch bag when Ben rang the bell at precisely seven-thirty.

Alice grabbed her keys from the bowl beside the door and ran down the stairs to meet Ben. He grinned when he saw her and took her hand in his. "Wow. You look beautiful." Alice blushed as he kissed her hand and opened the car door for her. She was tongue tied and couldn't think of a thing to say, so she slid into the passenger seat and busied herself with the seat belt as he walked around to the driver's side. The evening sun was still warm, so Ben had the roof down on his Audi TT. He put on his sunglasses and pulled away. "I thought we would go for a couple of drinks before dinner" He said, taking charge of the conversation. Alice nodded. Cross with herself that she felt so nervous. "There is a gorgeous little country pub not far from here that backs onto the river. I know the landlord."

"That sounds lovely," Alice said, glad to have found her voice at last. The journey lasted about half an hour, during which Ben did most of the talking. He told Alice about his plans to work his way up in his business and eventually run his own estate agency or property management company. He spoke about his friends in town and the volunteering he had been doing with local support groups recently. Alice found him fascinating. He was almost the total opposite of her. He was driven and ambitious and seemed to have his life mapped out. He had a plan and he knew where he wanted to be. She on the other hand liked to think of herself as more of a free spirit. She had always been creative and was always drawing, painting, or crafting something. She started a new project almost every week and often found herself totally absorbed in the process, sometimes working on a painting for days at a time, barely remembering to eat or sleep. Other times she would abandon a project midway through and go for weeks or months without looking at it again. She wondered what it must be like to know what you will be doing in five years or even five weeks' time. She had enrolled in University with the hope that working on her degree might be the thing that finally inspired her to focus on a career. At the very least she figured she could do an extra year after completing and train to be a teacher. She quite liked that idea in fact. She had always been good with kids. She liked their honesty and uncomplicated nature.

"Here we are" said Ben, rather unnecessarily, as they pulled up outside The Ferryman pub. Alice stepped out of the car and pulled her phone out of her bag to take some photos. The pub was a rickety looking thatched building, nestled against a chalk cliff. The river ran lazily alongside it and Alice could just see around the corner several rowing boats tied up against a wooden jetty. Several couples were enjoying their drinks at wooden tables dotted around the grounds. "This place is beautiful," she said, more to herself than anyone else. In her head she was planning a new fabric design based on the images she had just taken. When she had finished, Ben took her hand and led her over to a table underneath a wooden gazebo with a view up the river toward an old stone bridge. "What can I get you?" He asked her as she arranged herself on the wooden seat.

"Erm, a glass of wine would be nice please. White." While Ben left to go to the bar Alice took a couple more pictures, planning to paint the scene when she got a chance. The evening air was warm, and she felt totally content watching insects buzzing over the top of the water, occasionally being met by the hungry jaws of the fish lurking below.

The wine and the perfect late summer weather combined to relax Alice and make her feel more comfortable opening up to Ben. As the evening wore on, she found him more and more easy to talk to. After a couple of drinks at the pub they returned to town to their reservation at the Italian. Ben left his car at the office so he could share a bottle of wine with Alice. She was already feeling tipsy by the time the food arrived and was glad they were eating to soak up some of the alcohol. She was not a big drinker and she didn't want to show herself up on their first date. The food was delicious and the two of them chatted non-stop throughout the meal. Ben seemed to know everyone in there and Alice thought it was sweet that he made sure to say hello to everyone and asked about their family by name. To her it was evidence of how nice he was that so many people seemed to like him, and he showed genuine interest in everyone they met.

By the end of the evening Alice was pretty much smitten. Ben suggested that they take a walk along the seafront to sober up a little. They walked down onto the sand and took off their shoes to paddle in the warm, shallow water. Alice enjoyed the feeling of the sand sinking between her toes. She had never walked by the sea at night before and was mesmerised by the inky black of the water and the shards of silver from the moonlight on the surface. All she could hear was the gentle whoosh of the waves as they lapped around her ankles. Ben took her hand as they reached the wooden pier, and they climbed up to a low ledge and sat with their bare feet dangling over the side into the water. When Ben leaned over to kiss her, Alice melted into his embrace. She couldn't remember wanting anything more than she wanted him to hold her right then. The smell of the salt air mingling with the spicy scent of his aftershave was intoxicating. Every nerve in her body was tingling and she pressed against him, pulling him closer to her, surprised at her own boldness. Eventually, to her disappointment he pulled away and helped her up. "We should get back. Its late" he said, taking her hand and helping her across the stones to the promenade. They walked arm in arm along the river path into town and back to her flat, where Ben left Alice on the doorstep with a kiss. She could barely sleep that night as she kept reliving the evening over and over in her mind. Just a few short hours ago she had been alone, but suddenly something had clicked into place. She knew without doubt that she was in love. Not a lovestruck teenager kind of love, or even a lust filled fantasy love. She felt that when she met Ben there was a moment of recognition, as though something she had lost had just been found. Maybe this was what people meant when they talked about finding a soul mate.

The two of them met up every night that week. Alice had started her Uni course and was already falling behind by the first weekend. She was caught up in a whirlwind with Ben and she couldn't seem to slow it down. They went out every evening, returning to her flat in the early hours. She slept for a few hours then had to hop on a bus to be at her lessons by 9am. She had not expected the workload to be so high. So much for being eased into it. By Wednesday of the second week she decided she had to speak to Ben about it. She broached the subject that evening when they were eating out at yet another dazzlingly expensive restaurant.

"Ben, you know I love spending the evenings with you....," she started. "Uh oh," countered Ben, interrupting her "it sounds like there is a big old 'but' just about to enter this conversation".

Alice took his hands across the table. "I love spending the evenings with you......however, I need to concentrate on my studies. I am way behind the other students. I think it would be a good idea if we only saw each other at weekends. I need to get some work done, and I can't do that when we are out all the time. Not that I don't love it" she quickly added as she saw his face drop. Ben withdrew his hands and sat upright in his chair. "No problem. If you need more time alone that's fine," he said.

"Please don't be like that Ben, it's not that I want to be alone, I just need to get some work done. I moved here to concentrate on my art and I just haven't had time to do that." Alice tried to make her voice sound reasonable and calm, however she found his sulky face manipulative and annoying. "I said its fine, didn't I?" countered Ben. "Let's just get the bill so we can get out of here." Alice was properly annoyed now, but she decided to take the tactful approach rather than start an argument. "It's ok. Let's finish our meal. We can talk about this another day. I can catch up at Uni tomorrow. It's no big deal." She smiled at Ben and was pleased to see he was willing to let the conversation drop. She made a decision to look at her timetable tomorrow and factor in some extra time during the day to work on her assignments.

The next day Alice was working in her favourite art studio at the university. She had the place to herself, so she had plugged her phone into the whiteboard and was listening to music as loud as she dared without disturbing the class next door. It helped her concentrate and she soon found herself in the zone. She was working on a sculpture using clay, which was a new medium for her. She had never had a chance to work with it before as it was quite messy and needed a kiln and specialist paints that she had never had access to, so she was excited to see what she could produce. She was making an abstract work built over a chicken wire frame, which was a bold choice for a first effort. Happy hours passed, and it was only when the cleaner interrupted her by coming in and emptying the bin that she realised how late it was. Alice took a step back and looked at the work she had produced. She was pleased with the results and couldn't wait to get started on painting it. She carried the piece to the drying room before removing her apron and washing her hands, which were thick with dry clay. She realised she was starving and tried to think back when she had last had anything to eat. That would be the meal she had eaten at the Chinese the previous night. She realised that was over 19 hours ago, so she headed over to the canteen to pick up something to eat.

Sitting down with her meal Alice finally took her phone out of her bag to check her messages. She was dismayed to find 29 missed calls and a bunch of text messages from Ben, all sounding increasingly more anxious for her to call. She called him back immediately, worried that something awful had happened while she had been obliviously playing with clay. He picked up on the second ring. "Ben, what's wrong? Are you ok?" she started before he cut her off, talking over her. "Where have you been, I have been so worried!" His tone was verging on angry, which Alice found confusing. "I've been at Uni, working. I told you I was behind..." She said. Ben was not ready to calm down and her confusion irritated him. "I have been worried sick. You didn't answer your phone all day. I didn't know where you were or if something had happened. I haven't been able to concentrate, thinking something had happened to you."

Alice decided enough was enough and tried to steer the conversation onto another topic. "I'm sorry I didn't get your messages, but I was in the zone, and I didn't have my phone with me. Its sweet that you worried, but I'm a big girl. I can take care of myself. Let's not argue about it. How about you pick me up from here and we can go for a walk?" She heard Ben huff at the end of the line.

"Ok, if it's not going to get in the way of your work" he said, sounding gruff. Alice thought she heard a note of sarcasm but chose to take the sentiment at face value. "No, it's fine, I'm finished for the day. I am just going to eat, then I will be down. Give me twenty minutes." Ben agreed and put the phone down. Alice went back to her meal but found that she was not that hungry after all. The contentment she had felt ten minutes ago had been replaced by a feeling of irritation. She knew that Ben was just concerned about her, and it was sweet that he was worried, but she didn't want to have to deal with him behaving like a petulant teenager whenever she had to work late.

By the time Ben arrived, just over twenty minutes later, he was back to his usual, charming self. He waited beside the car for Alice to come out, gathering her in his arms and kissing her neck. His lips were warm on her chilled skin and Alice melted into his embrace; all memories of his previous snippiness forgotten. They drove a short way along the coast, enjoying the colours of the setting sun reflecting in the windows of the houses lining the road. Ben pulled up in a gravel car park, next to an old lighthouse, and climbed out to open the door for Alice. Ben opened the boot and pulled out a chilled bottle of prosecco and two plastic champagne flutes. Hand in hand they tramped across the gravel and onto the sand dunes that surrounded the lighthouse. They were on a chalk cliff, that while not particularly high, gave them a stunning panoramic view of the sea and the beach below. The sun was dropping rapidly now toward the horizon bathing everything in a pink light. They sat for two hours or more as the sky darkened, turning the sea into an inky expanse. After the first glass of prosecco Ben switched to water as he was driving, but somehow the bottle was empty by the time the air had chilled enough to encourage them to leave. Alice had to hold on tightly to Ben as they followed their footsteps back across the dunes as the alcohol and air combined to make her head spin in a rather delicious way. She stumbled on a tuffet of sharp grass and toppled to the ground, dragging Ben with her. She giggled as he landed on top of her and pulled him in for a kiss.

The next morning Alice woke up late. The sun was already

streaming in through her half-drawn curtains. She held her hand up to her eyes to block out the light, which was causing a stabbing headache. Fumbling around on the bedside table she was grateful to find a glass of water and a packet of paracetamol waiting there for her. She popped two out of the packet and drank half the water in one mouthful. She waited a couple of seconds to test if that was going to come back up, before downing the rest of the drink. Running her fingers through her hair Alice realised she had a headful of sand. It was all over her pillow and in the bed, and now she was aware of it, it was making her itch. She couldn't go back to sleep now, so she dragged herself into the shower.

The water did its job and by the time she was dressed, Alice was starting to feel much more human. She rarely drank, and now she was beginning to remember why. She was a total lightweight. She did a quick memory check to make sure she could remember how the evening had ended. The two of them had made love for the first time on the sand dune. She could feel every touch of his hand on her skin. Ben had been reluctant at first, not wanting to take advantage of her, but the alcohol had made her bold and she had assured him she was ready, rolling over so he was on his back and she was astride him. The dunes were dark and starting to get damp in the cooling air, which had felt great against the heat of their bodies. They had lain there for a long while afterwards, wrapped in the picnic blanket, watching the stars floating across the night sky. It was the early hours by they had returned to her flat. They had made love again before falling into a deep sleep.

Alice checked her phone. Ben had called several times before giving up and sending her a text that simply said "Had an amazing night. See you this evening. B xx" She tried to call him back, but it went to voicemail. He was obviously with a client. She would try again later. Alice stripped the bed and gathered up all the bedding, which she put into the washing machine before making herself her favourite hangover breakfast of dippy eggs and brown toast soldiers with an extra strong cup of coffee. After hanging out the laundry she spent a productive morning working on a new painting inspired by the light and the stars of the previous evening. She was pleased with the way it came out. The creativity had just flowed through her and the picture was completed by the time Ben came to pick her up again early that evening.

After sharing a pizza and watching a dodgy 80s romcom, Alice took Ben into the bedroom where she had displayed her new painting on an easel in the corner of the room. "Wow, that is beautiful," he said. "It reminds me of last night," Alice grinned. "It's supposed to. Pictures are like a diary. They are filled with all your memories and emotions, the same as a poem or a journal." Ben put his arm around her and pulled her close to him. "I never thought of art like that before. Sort of makes sense," he said. "We should put that picture above our bed. Then we will always be reminded of our first time."

Alice propped herself up on one elbow. "What do you mean *our* bed?" she asked. Ben knocked her off balance and laid her back down to kiss her face. "What I mean..." he said, whilst covering her in kisses, ".......is, let's move in together." He stopped and pulled away to look at her face. Alice thought about it for a few seconds. This was crazy. She had known him less than a fortnight. She hardly knew anything about him. He could be an axe-murderer for all she knew. And what would people think of her? She threw her arms around his neck "Yes, lets," she said.

Three days later, Ben had moved into the flat with her. Alice had wondered if she might regret the decision, but it was working out great. They could spend a lot more time together and she was still able to keep up with everyone else on her course. She had even had time to join the local theatre group, helping out with painting the backdrops. One of the other women on her course was acting in their next production and had got chatting to Alice about it one morning. They were putting on a performance of The Sound of Music and needed someone to produce sets and props for them. Alice had jumped at the chance to paint on a huge canvas and had used the paintings she had done recently of the country pub as her inspiration. She was so proud of the result that she was planning to enter it as part of her portfolio.

Alice had made some new friends at the theatre group. In particular, she was enjoying the company of Maya. Alice was drawn to her confidence and vivaciousness. She was playing Maria, and had an angelic singing voice that Alice felt she could listen to all day. Alice found it funny to hear Maya in character talking sweetly, then to hear her in her normal voice effing and blinding all over the place. Maya exuded life and energy and wasn't scared of anything. She was the polar opposite of Alice, which Alice believed was probably why they got on so well. One evening, after a particularly fun rehearsal, Alice invited Maya back to the flat for a drink. Ben was on the sofa in the lounge watching a football game. "Hi Ben, this is Maya, Maya, Ben.," she said by way of introduction. "Don't worry, we won't disturb your game. We will go and sit in the kitchen." She took Maya's arm to lead the way, but Ben had shut off the TV and was on his feet. "Nonsense," he said with his charming smile, "It was a boring game anyway. Come and sit down." He took Maya's hand and shook it, then patted the seat next to him. "Nice to meet you Maya. Are you related to Pamela Young?" he asked.

"Actually, yes. She's my Mum" replied Maya. "How do you know her?"

"I used to wait tables in your Mum's restaurant when I was doing my A Levels." Ben smiled, lost in memories. "She's an excellent Chef, your Mum. And a lovely woman. Say Hi to her for me." Before Maya had the chance to reply, Alice was back with the wine and three glasses. She poured them all drinks while Ben put some music on in the background. Alice was pleased that Ben and Maya seemed to be getting on well. They had a lot to talk about as Ben knew her family from years back. Eventually the

80

conversation turned to relationships. "So, Maya, are you seeing anyone?" asked Ben. "Sadly not." Maya replied, staring into her wine glass. "Ah, so there is someone you want to be with then" said Ben with a cheeky grin.

"Stop it Ben She doesn't want to talk about it obviously". Said Alice, always the first to rescue a difficult conversation. Maya looked up. "It's ok Alice, I don't mind. There is someone I like, but he doesn't want me unfortunately, so that's fine." She had a stoic look on her face that belied the sadness beneath. "That is definitely not fine," said Ben with a drunken wave of his arm. "That's criminal. A beautiful, sexy woman like you and he turns you down? He must be mad. Or gay." Maya gave a little giggle. "He's not gay. Or mad for that matter. It just can't happen. But thank you for saying I'm beautiful." She looked him in the eye, and he returned her gaze. "Oh dear, we are out of wine," interrupted Alice. She was starting to feel uncomfortable and the alcohol was making her tired. "It's late. Shall I call you a taxi Maya?"

"No need," said Ben getting up from the sofa. "I will walk her home. Fresh air will do me good." Alice looked to Maya to see if she was ok with that and gathered her cardigan and handbag for her. "See you at the next rehearsal," she said, giving Maya a hug goodbye. "Yes, thanks for a lovely evening." Maya replied, before stepping out of the door to catch up with Ben who had already left without her. Alice closed the door behind them and went upstairs to brush her teeth. She climbed into bed with the intention of waiting for Ben, but within minutes she was sound asleep.

The following weeks passed in a blur. Alice was happy. Ben was kind and thoughtful and told her every night before they fell asleep all the things that he loved about her.

Alice finished her first semester at University ahead of the rest of the class, and Ben was promoted at work. The two of them decided to take a few days off from working and studying at Christmas to recoup some energy and focus on each other. Alice loved that Ben planned time like that into their lives. He seemed to enjoy spending time with her, listening to her talk or just watching tv with her. He was devoted to her in a way she hadn't realised existed outside of films or books. Christmas Eve was their first day off together so they planned to have a long lay in and a lazy walk into town for breakfast at the pub, but Alice woke early and couldn't get back to sleep. She lay there for a little while listening to Ben snore, before finally giving up and going to make coffee. She couldn't put her finger on what was making her feel so restless. She usually slept like a log. Recently she had been feeling exhausted, barely able to keep her eyes open in the evening. Often in the past few weeks she had fallen asleep on the sofa in the evening, only to be woken up by Ben telling her to go to bed.

Alice took her coffee back to the bedroom and settled down to read. The smell of the coffee on the table next to her was nauseating. She wondered if the milk was on the turn. It had smelled ok, but maybe it had curdled in the hot water. She took the cup into the bathroom and threw the drink down the sink. As the smell hit her nose her stomach flipped, and she threw up in the toilet. She felt better almost immediately and went back to bed, snuggling up against Ben. She must have dozed back off to sleep as when she awoke the bed was empty and she could smell breakfast cooking. She realised she was starving so she threw her dressing gown on and wandered through to the living room. "Morning sleepyhead" said Ben from where he was crouched behind the sofa. "What on earth are you doing?" said Alice. Ben stood up and wiped his dusty hands on his trousers. "Making way for the Christmas tree. I thought we could put it up in the window. I just need to get this sofa over to the wall, but I didn't realise how heavy it is. Grab that end, will you?" Alice did as she was asked and between the two of them, they half lifted, and half dragged the heavy sofa to its temporary new position. "I didn't think we were going to bother with decorations and stuff," said Alice. "That's more a kids thing really. Anyway, I don't even have a tree, so that's the end of that." Ben was having none of it. "Of course we are having a tree. And crackers and fairy lights and egg nog. Actually, what even is egg nog? We can go shopping today and get everything we need. There's a Christmas market not far from here," he finished triumphantly, taking her hand, and pulled her down onto the sofa next to him. Alice knew when she was beaten. "Ok, fine," she said, leaning in to kiss him as she stood up. "But I need coffee if we are going to do this". Ben fetched her a cup from the kitchen, along with a bacon sandwich. "This is our first Christmas together. I want it to be special." Ben said. He was looking at Alice with those puppy eyes. She felt guilty for being so anti it. It was not his fault. Christmas had been a terrible time for her when she was a kid. Not something to celebrate. Her parents both struggled with addiction of one sort or another. Her Dad would finish work on Christmas eve and go straight to the pub with his mates, where he would stay until closing time. Often, he didn't make it home until the early hours of Christmas morning. He would then spend the day with a massive hangover and in a foul mood. Her parents refused to row in front of her, instead they would sit in frosty silence, refusing to look each other in the eye. Mum would spend much of the morning in the kitchen cooking the roast, which she was then too angry or upset to eat. She popped painkillers to take the edge off the day and often spent most of the afternoon sleeping off their effects. By the time Alice was ten years old her parents were gone, and she was stuck with her aunt Emma, who spent Christmas in the pub or shacked up with her latest boyfriend. Alice spent most of her Christmases in her room, where she would paint and listen to music. If things were bad she would take off on her bike with a packed lunch and spend the day in the park, watching the families out for a walk, children riding new bikes or scooters or pushing new dolls in toy prams. It had been a long time since she had thought of Christmas with anything other than a feeling of dread in the pit of her stomach.

The day was cold and there was the threat of snow in the air, which added to the atmosphere at the Christmas market. Alice had never been to one before, preferring to avoid anything to do with the season. The air was filled with the spicy, warm scent of the hot glühwein that was served from giant copper kettles. People wandered around with paper cups of the strong-smelling drink, even though it was barely noon. Ben bought them one each, and though Alice was not much of a drinker she enjoyed the warm feeling it gave her, and she began to relax and enjoy herself. She was fascinated by the beautiful hand-crafted gifts and ornaments, and spent a while picking out a hand painted silk scarf which she thought would be a perfect gift for Maya. Ben led her toward the Christmas tree lot where he picked out one of the biggest trees they had. She couldn't help but be infected by his enthusiasm, and although the tree would take up a huge space in the flat, she agreed to him buying it and gave her address to the stallholder who kindly agreed to deliver it to them that evening. Once the tree was in the bag the pair of them headed toward a seating area in the middle of the courtyard, where they ate a lunch of German hotdogs followed by chocolate covered strawberries. To Ben's delight Alice went to purchase drinks and returned with two cups of steaming egg nog.

Alice was starting to enjoy herself. Now they had bought the tree she thought they might as well decorate it. She spent way too much on a set of tree lights and a lovely Nordic garland. She picked up a hand blown glass ornament, with gold stars fused into it, that she thought would be the perfect embellishment for the top of the tree, but when she looked at the price she sadly had to leave it and walk away. She decided she could make her own tree topper instead. As the afternoon began to darken, there was a definite chill in the air. The lights were turned on in all the little market cabins, adding a magical glow to the event. They picked up another glass of glühwein and found a seat next to the open-air ice rink, where they could watch the skaters enjoying the winter fun. Alice was glad to take the weight off her feet. They had been walking around all day and her ankles felt like they were swelling up. She put her feet up on the chair in front of her. "I just need to pop to the loo" said Ben "will you be alright here for a minute?" Alice continued to watch the skaters, mesmerized. "Of course, take you time." Ben wrapped his arms around her from behind and kissed her hair. "I might wander back over to the doughnut stand as well then. Back in a bit" Alice waved her hand behind her. She didn't want him to see the tears in her eyes as he might mistake them for sadness. She didn't know if it was the alcohol, or the magical atmosphere of the market, but she couldn't remember ever being this happy. She didn't want to move or speak, in case the moment ended, and the feeling passed.

It was dark by the time they got home and unloaded all their bags from the back of the taxi. There were even a few flakes of snow in the air. Alice surprised herself by realising that she hoped it would snow. She normally hated the stuff. It was usually just an inconvenience to her. It was cold and slushy and made everywhere slippery and uncomfortable. Right now, though, she thought how romantic it would be to wake in the morning to a fresh covering of snow, purifying the town and burying it under a layer of white. She must be drunk, she laughed to herself.

They had barely got in the door before a van pulled up and two men knocked on their door with their Christmas tree. It seemed even larger once it was in the lobby and the men were glad there was a lift to save them having to carry it all the way up the stairs. They were very helpful, even going as far as to unwrap the tree from its bindings and making sure it was secure in its metal base before they left. Alice offered them a drink, but they turned her down as they had several deliveries to get through before they could go home to their families. Feeling generous, Alice took two bottles of wine from the rack and handed one each to the men and wished them a Happy Christmas. As they left Ben teased her. "Look at you getting in the Christmas spirit.

Isn't that nice". Alice would usually respond with a sarcastic comment or joke, but today she decided not to rise to it. "Actually," she said "Yes, it is nice. Thank you for today" She wrapped her arms around him, and they kissed for a long minute. Pulling away from him finally she said "No time for that. This tree is not going to decorate itself you know!" She thrust the box of lights into his hands. "You sort out the lights, I will sort out the wine" Ben agreed and started to unbox the lights as Alice headed to the kitchen to find wine glasses.

Alice stood back to admire their efforts. The tree smelt wonderful, permeating the flat with its woodland scent. The lights twinkled and glowed against the gold highlights of the garland she had expertly wound around the tree. She had added some bows of green, red, and gold ribbon that she had in her craft box and was pleased with the result. "The only thing missing is a star" said Ben as he produced an expertly wrapped box from behind his back. "Merry first Christmas Alice". She took the box and lifted the lid to find the blown glass tree topper nestled among tissue paper. Tears once again filled her eyes, which this time she allowed Ben to see. "Its beautiful Ben, thank you" she cried. He took it from her and clambered up on to the arm of the sofa to place it on the top of the tree over the topmost fairy light, which lit it up from inside with a warm glow. Alice was delighted with it.

The two of them sat in the darkened living room enjoying a glass of wine and watching the snow fall gently outside. Alice was just starting to doze, her head leaning against Ben's shoulder, when he moved and startled her awake. "It's past midnight" He said, pushing her shoulder gently until she was sitting upright. "It's officially Christmas, which means I can give you your present now." He disappeared from the room for a minute and returned with a small box, wrapped with a red bow. Alice took the parcel, pulled the bow, and lifted the lid off the top. The box opened like flower, revealing a small, glass Christmas bauble nestled inside. The surface of the glass shimmered with hints of red and gold. A heart shaped plaque on the front of it was embossed with their initials. Alice was touched. "Now it makes sense why you wanted to get a Christmas tree," she laughed, leaning in to kiss him. She lifted the bauble up on its silk hanger and it twirled round with the movement, revealing it was hollow with an open back. Dangling from a decorative ribbon inside the bauble was a gold engagement ring with a large, solitaire diamond. Alice gasped and nearly dropped the bauble. She looked back toward Ben, who was already on one knee. Her free hand flew instinctively to her mouth to stifle an excited yelp. "Alice Sheppard, will you make me the happiest man in the world and do me the honour of becoming my wife?" He said. Alice pretended to think about it for a few seconds, before telling him that yes, of course she would marry him. He put the ring on her finger, and they kissed under the tree. Maybe Christmas was not so bad after all.

CHAPTER 14
MAGGIE 2019

Maggie could barely contain her excitement that morning as she made herself a hasty breakfast of coffee and toast. Alice had invited her along to the playgroup with her this morning, and she had jumped at the chance as she knew it would be a great opportunity to meet Maya and Freddie. Maggie already felt as if she knew them so she would have to be careful to play it cool and not let slip any details that gave the game away if she didn't want to risk scaring them off. She didn't want Maya to know that she had been monitoring her social media pages for over a year now, as she knew it could freak her out. She knew from Maya's Instagram page that she was into Harry Potter, so Maggie had bought herself a Slytherin House t-shirt to wear. She hoped it would be a good conversation starter. She had arranged to meet Alice at the coffee shop in town before they headed off together to the library, where the playgroup met in the children's area. She arrived 15 minutes early, so she ordered herself a latte and took a seat outside to wait. It was a chilly day, but the sun was out soaking the town with a buttery warmth. She closed her eyes and turned her face to the sun to take in the morning rays. Lottie broke the peace while she was still a good distance away. "Aunty Aggie" She called. Maggie smiled at the cute nickname that had evolved recently. She crouched down and opened her arms for Lottie to run into. The shy little girl had almost disappeared, replaced instead with an increasingly more confident young lady. Maggie hugged her tight, then moved over to kiss Archie hello. He gurgled and smiled at her from behind his dummy in a way that made her womb ache with longing.

Alice kissed Maggie hello and tasked her with watching the children while she went inside to order, taking Maggie's travel cup with her to refill with fresh coffee. Carrying their fresh drinks, the pair of them sauntered along the road to the Library children's room. Before they had travelled more than three hundred metres, a loud, confident sounding voice could be heard calling Alice. They stopped where they were and waited for the woman to catch up. Maggie could tell even from this distance that it was Maya. She was almost a foot taller than Maggie at 6 feet and had a mane of luxurious honey-blonde hair to top her off. Even wearing jeans and trainers with an old check shirt, she pulled off an elegance that Maggie would not be able to with a full makeover and six months of training. She was pushing a smart, blue pushchair in which Freddie was sleeping, snuggled up with his stuffed dinosaur. He had a halo of soft white hair fanning out around his head.

As Maya came alongside them, she pulled Alice in for a hug and kissed her on the cheek. In one fluid movement she crouched down to kiss Lottie on the head and hefted Archie from his buggy, rubbing noses with him and making him giggle. She pulled him close to her and sniffed the top of his head, breathing him in deeply. "That baby smell is delicious," she exclaimed. "I could eat him up." She upended the boy who rewarded her with further giggles of delight. Alice waited until Maya had finished her hellos before introducing her to Maggie. "Oh, you're the one who has been keeping my friend busy are you?" Maya said. Her eyes twinkled with a spark of fun when she said it, but Maggie thought she could detect a slight note of resentment there. "Not at all, Alice has been showing me around. I just moved here. To a flat. By the river. And the car broke down, so I gave her a lift, and then the babysitter didn't turn up, so...." Maggie couldn't stop herself talking. She knew she was coming across as an idiot, but she found herself suddenly nervous. "Anyway. I'll shut up now" She turned away abruptly and pretended to read a text to hide her embarrassment. Maya brushed the moment away. "I can see you are a Harry Potter fan, so I will let you off this time." She turned back toward Alice, "So Sweetie, I have the best news, look at this!" She thrust her mobile phone with a picture of her fundraising site with its full totalizer into Alice's face. "Can you believe it? We have raised way more than the target now." Alice grabbed Maya with both arms and started jumping up and down in a circle with her. Maggie held her breath, sure that at any minute one of them would read the name out and guess it was her who had given the money. She wished she had thought to use a false account. If they were to click on her profile picture it would be obvious that Maggie Crossford, was her. The two women were alternately screaming and laughing, with Lottie looking on in bemusement. They were loud enough to wake Freddie, who immediately wanted to be let out of his harness to join Lottie on the pavement.

Alice demanded that her friend tell her all about what she planned to spend the extra funds on, which Maya was more than happy to do. It was clear that the two of them had not seen each other for a while and had a lot to catch up on. Maggie contented herself to walk behind with the children. She was touched by how close Lottie and Freddie appeared to be. The held hands as they walked and Lottie was humming a song, occasionally throwing a few words in here and there. Freddie appeared content to just wander along with her, listening to the melody.

They arrived at the library a few minutes before everyone else, so they stowed their pushchairs in the atrium and wandered through to the seating area. Alice hung back to speak to a man wearing a council lanyard, that Maggie assumed to be one of the leaders of the group. Maya led the three children to seats at the back of the circle. Once they were seated Maggie pulled up a beanbag alongside them and looked around the room trying to find something to make conversation about. Alice could be heard laughing at something that her companion had said, though Maggie couldn't make out any words. "So, how long have you known Alice?" she said. It was a bit of a feeble opener, but the best she could do under the circumstances. Maya was distracted, keeping one eye on Lottie and Freddie while soothing a fussing Alfie. "About five year's, I think. I met her at a theatre group, just after she moved here." Maggie nodded slightly, that fitted with what she already knew. Maya had been enrolled in a musical theatre course in 2015. "She wasn't in the play though was she." Maya raised her eyebrows and glanced at Maggie from the side of her eyes. "No, she was a painter, I was a singer. How did you know she was not performing?" Maggie silently cursed herself. Two sentences into the conversation and she had already slipped up. "I just guessed. I mean you seem like totally different people; it makes sense you would be doing different things" She blustered. It was a weak response and she knew it. She spoke quickly to move the conversation on. "So how did you meet then? If you don't mind me asking?"

Alfie had stopped fussing and was seated happily on the floor in front of Maya, chewing on the dummy clip that was attached to his clothing. Maya took a minute to reply. "We were both involved in the first-year production of The Sound of Music. She was painting the scenery. She did an amazing job. She's so talented. We've been friends since then I suppose" Maya shuffled over then and patted the seat next to her for Alice to sit down. "Thanks" said Alice. "Oliver says Hi" Maya shook her head slightly. "Why do you still talk to him. He's such a loser. We hate him remember!" Alice rolled her eyes. "I don't remember agreeing to that. He's nice Maya. You should give him a chance. He asked about you again." Maya frowned a shot a glare in his direction. "I hope you told him to sod off." Maggie watched this interaction with interest and wondered what Oliver had done to offend Maya. He seemed pleasant enough, and he was certainly attractive. He was tall and slender with a boyish face and slightly too long hair that curled over the tops of his ears in an endearing way. He caught her looking at him and flashed her a smile. Embarrassed, she turned back to the conversation between the two women. Alice was explaining to Maya how Maggie had helped her with the car when they first met. Maggie was struck by the difference between the two women. Alice was quietly spoken, and although pretty, she tended to blend in with her surroundings. Maggie couldn't think of any situation that Maya would blend into. She had a presence that would fill the room.

Other mums and children were starting to arrive now. Most of them seemed to know each other, and Alice made a point of introducing them all to Maggie. Maggie was usually totally comfortable talking to strangers, and could chat to anyone, but sitting next to Maya made her oddly nervous and tongue tied. She had a vague feeling that Maya was watching her, assessing her. She was glad once the group leader sat down and the session started. It transpired that Oliver was there to provide the music. He sat just outside of the circle where a keyboard was set up that Maggie had not even noticed. The group started by singing some well-known children's songs. Freddie and Lottie were loving it and knew every word to the songs by heart. Maggie noticed that Freddie tired much quicker than the other children did, and about halfway through the session he sat on his mum's lap with a thumb in his mouth happy to watch the others dance around him. He was still singing along to the songs around his thumb and was fighting to keep his eyes open. Maggie found him absolutely adorable and longed to scoop him up in her arms and hug him while he slept.

Twenty minutes later Oliver put away the keyboard and the other leaders dragged a big box of toys into the middle of the room. Most of the adults left the circle and gathered in groups around the room while the children played together on the floor. Alice was once again chatting to someone on the other side of the room, leaving Maya alone to watch the children. She was rocking Alfie to sleep in her arms, so Maggie took the opportunity to try talking to her again. "I didn't realise how popular she is" Maggie indicated in Alice's general direction with her eyes. Maya followed her gaze. "That's Mary Bosworth. She is one of Bens Bitches. I don't know why Alice puts up with her. She's too nice for her own good," she snorted. "Ben's Bitches?" Maggie asked. Maya turned to look her in the eye. "Have you met Ben yet? He's kinda hot." Maggie nodded. She didn't like the man, but she had to agree with Maya's appraisal of him. "Anyway" Maya continued "He has all these hangers on from the council and the school boards and different things he is involved in. They are just waiting for him to give them the nod and they will be all over him. It's pathetic really, sad old bags. I wouldn't stand for it myself." Maya strode away to place Alfie gently back in his pushchair. Maggie watched how gentle she was with him as she laid him down and stroked his hair. To speak to her she was all spikes and hard edges, you could easily believe this softer side didn't exist.

Maya returned with the pushchair, and sat on one of the hard, plastic seats dotted around the room. She crossed her legs and gently pushed the baby back and forth with her foot. "The secret is to never let the wheels stop moving" She laughed. "My mum always says that. Good bit of advice that." Maggie nodded in agreement, glad that Maya had introduced her mother into the conversation. "Wise woman your Mother." Maya pulled a face. "Well I wouldn't go as far as to call her wise. She does like giving advice though. Whether you want it or not." She pulled out her phone and started to scroll through messages. Maggie was desperate to keep the conversation going. "What does your mum do?" She knew that Maya's mum was called Pamela, and although she was only in her early fifties she was already retired. Her husband, Graham was an architect and the two of them had been together over twenty years. "Why do you want to know?" asked Maya. Maggie was a bit taken aback by Maya's direct response. She didn't think Maya was being unpleasant, she just wanted to know why Maggie was interested. Maggie liked that. It was refreshing to speak to someone who didn't appear to filter her responses at all. She decided a direct answer was the best response. "Just being nosey really. I don't know anyone here, so I'm just interested" Maya gave her an appraising look. She obviously decided she was happy with Maggie's answer as she relaxed and started chatting about her parents. She lived with them in a separate flat that they had built in outbuildings in the garden once she had told them she was pregnant with Freddie. "And what about the Father?" Maggie asked, aware that she was pushing her luck. "Where was he during all of this?"

"He was nowhere. He doesn't matter." Maya replied. Maggie pushed a bit further. "Does that mean you don't know who the father is?" Maya gave a short laugh. "Bloody hell, you don't hold back do you?" She paused for a moment. Maggie got the feeling she was debating telling her to piss off. "No, it doesn't mean that at all. I know who the father is, I just don't think it would be good for Freddie, or for me, if he was here interfering. Me and Freddie are fine on our own thanks." Maya picked her phone up and scrolled through messages, indicating that the conversation was over for now.

Alice managed to release herself from the grip of Mary Bosworth and scooped up Lottie on her way back. "Shall we go?" She suggested. Both women agreed that they had had enough, and it was a good time to leave. On the spur of the moment Maggie invited the two women up to her flat for lunch. Before she knew what she was saying, she had suggested they walk back along the river and have tea and sandwiches on her balcony. She had been baking yesterday afternoon, practicing recipes for the tearoom and was keen to have someone to try them out on. Lottie was the first to respond, with a rallying call for tea at Aunty Aggie's. The other two women quickly agreed, and they headed out together toward Maggie's home.

It had warmed up since the morning so Maggie opened the balcony doors and dragged some chairs out there so the three of them could sit and watch the boats on the river while they ate their lunch. She didn't have much furniture or any toys to keep the kids amused, so she improvised by giving the older two and empty packing box and a roll of bubble wrap to play with. They were having a great time playing make believe, while Alfie was sat on the floor with a wooden spoon and upturned saucepan for a drum.

She had been a bit nervous at first, inviting the two women into her home. She had very little furniture and had brought so few things with her when she moved that the place appeared sterile and lifeless. There were no pictures or ornaments as she had not wanted to bring anything at all that reminded her of her old life with Daniel. If Maya and Alice had noticed the lack of décor, they were too polite to say anything. Maggie realised they had probably just assumed she had not had a chance to unpack yet. She made a note to herself to go online that evening and order some furniture. If she was going to have visitors in, she ought to try to make the place look like a home.

She carried a full tray of cherry scones and pistachio macarons out to the balcony and set them down on the table to a round of oohs and aahs from the ladies. "These look great" said Maya. "Alice tells me you are planning to open a tearoom. Is that what you did before you moved here?"

"Well I have been thinking about it. We looked at a place yesterday that could be perfect" Said Alice, deliberately avoiding talking about the past. "I have made an appointment to view it tomorrow. Exciting stuff."

Alice grinned at her new friend. "That's great news. What time are you going?"

"I said I would meet him there at 9.30." replied Maggie "I was kinda hoping you would come with me. I mean, it's only fair, you did find it."

Alice jumped out of her seat. "Yes, I would love to," she said. "Maya you must come too" she looked to Maggie, "If you don't mind of course. Look at me just taking over."

"Of course I don't mind. The more the merrier." Both women looked expectantly toward Maya, who rolled her eyes at them. "Well someone needs to be the voice of reason I suppose. I can't let you two go bouncing in there like two excited puppies. You're bound to get ripped off on your own." Maggie conceded that she had a point. She was pleased that Maya appeared to be warming to her. She was struck with inspiration. "Maya, I was thinking about opening in the evening sometimes, for special events. Like maybe a Jazz evening or a charity event. I'm going to need a singer. I wondered if you might be interested?" Maya looked almost shocked. She studied Maggie's face, eyebrows raised, trying to work out if she was serious. Maggie nodded to reassure her that she meant what she had just said and watched two small dimples appear on Maya's perfect face as she smiled her acceptance. "I would love to. Thanks for asking me." Maya said with a smile. She was flattered. "I will definitely have to make sure this place is any good now wont I."

Before leaving the flat, they made plans to meet in the morning. Freddie and Lottie would be at day-care, so Alice made arrangements for Alfie to stay with Ben's mum to give her the morning to herself. A little later, as Maggie saw them all to the door, she couldn't believe her luck. Not only had she met Maya, but she had already made a friend of her. She had dreamed of this day, never believing that it would happen. Maya was everything she had hoped her to be, and more. If only Daniel could see her now.

Maggie woke bright and early the next morning. She had barely slept all night, plans for the tearoom spinning round in her mind. She had done a quick check of her finances. Now she had tenants in the house she had a reasonable chunk of money to spend on having the building and decorating work done on the building assuming that there were no nasty surprises when they viewed it later that day. She wasn't due to meet the girls for another hour, so she made a cup of tea and took it out to the balcony to drink while searching on the internet for local suppliers of the produce she would need.

An hour later Maggie had a list of businesses to call to arrange meetings with. She took her empty cup inside, picked up her handbag and keys, and set off on foot to the old lifeboat station. Maya was already there, peering through the windows as Alice and Maggie had done the day before. She turned when she heard Maggie approaching. "I have to say, I thought you were a bit bonkers when you mentioned this place yesterday, but its bloody awesome," she said by way of a greeting. Maggie was pleased at her reaction. "Morning Maya. Now imagine sitting out here with a crab sandwich and a cup of tea, looking out to sea."

"Sounds perfect" said Ben, coming around the side of the building with Alice a step behind him. "How about we get inside and get these doors open?" Everyone said hello and followed Ben in through the normal sized front door, into a small lobby area where there were hooks on the wall for coats and a big shoe rack. Another door led through into the large space where the lifeboat had been kept. Maya was pleased to see that the interior was in very good repair. There was a concrete floor that was painted dark green and the walls were exposed brick. Around both sides of the room and along the back was an observation balcony, which Maggie thought would be fantastic as an extra seating area. Even as it was the building would not look out of place in a fashionable magazine.

There were stairs at the back of the main room, which led up to the balcony. A door in the back wall led through to what must have been the equipment room. One wall was fitted with lockers and a long bench with hooks above, obviously for changing clothes. The other side of the room held a small kitchen area, next to a toilet and shower room. The four of them inspected the whole place thoroughly, taking pictures on their phones. Ben had brought a copy of the details for the dimensions of the building. Once they had all had a good look they gathered at the front door. "Well ladies. What do we think?" said Ben, who had realised quickly that he was not just selling to Maggie. Alice and Maya's opinions seemed to be an important part of the decision process. The three women looked at each other, before Maya made the first move. "I fucking love it. It's perfect. I can already see it full of people," she gushed. Maggie looked to Alice, who agreed with Maya. "It could be great. I really like the trendy, boho vibe of it. There's a lot of potential in there." All eyes turned to Maggie, who was looking thoughtful. "I liked it. It shouldn't be too much work to put an industrial kitchen in there. The electrics and water all look ok. We might need to do something about the heating, but I am thinking a log burner would be great in the middle of the space, or even an open fire..." Her voice trailed away as she was lost in thought. Ben looked around the group. They were all clearly excited about the idea, they just needed a nudge. "Do you know what I have always thought this town needs is a community hub," he said, watching the women's reactions to what he was saying. He had sparked their attention. "Somewhere for women to meet up and talk about their day, somewhere for community groups to meet and share a sandwich. Somewhere even for the elderly to meet up and get a bit of company and see a friendly face." He could see in Maggie's eyes that he was on the right track. "We need a place for anyone who is lonely to get together with friends. Plus of course, this place would be a total tourist trap in the Summer. If you play your cards right, this could be *the* venue of Smallhaven."

All three women exchanged glances. Maggie could almost feel the excitement buzzing from the two friends standing in front of her. "We'll take it," she told Ben, nodding her head in triumph. Maya screamed and hopped over to fling her arms around Maggie in a bear hug that almost squeezed the breath out of her. Alice joined in and the three of them jumped in a little circle until they were interrupted by Ben asking Maggie to join him at the agency. "Sure. Thanks. I will be there in twenty minutes," she said. "I'll meet you there."

"Well, I think you are on to a winner. Congratulations," said Ben, the picture of charm as he put his muscled arms around Maggie for a celebratory hug. "I will see you at the office shortly. Lovely doing business with you." With that he gave Alice a kiss on the mouth, hopped into his car and left in a shower of stones as he wheel span onto the road. Maggie looked at the two women in front of her and past them to the large room that she had just committed to turning into a business. "No going back now. Greatness or bust," she said with a flourish.

CHAPTER 15
ALICE 2016

Alice's tutor called her over as she was about to leave the class. It was halfway through the new term at Uni, and Alice loved it. She waved her friend off and stepped back to speak to her favourite teacher. "Alice, I just wanted to tell you how impressed I am with your last piece. Your skills are developing beautifully. People are starting to take notice." Alice put her hand on her chest, flattered. She hoped she was not blushing. "Thank you, Sarah. That means such a lot coming from you. I feel so much more confident now." Sarah sat on the edge of the desk and gave Alice an appraising look. "Some of the other academics and I are impressed with the risks you are taking with your work. So much so, that we would like to offer you the chance to paint a piece for the next show we put on in a few months' time." Alice didn't know what to say. This was bigger than she could have imagined. First year students were never chosen for the University exhibition. "I'm flattered. That is so…" She didn't know what to say, so she just smiled and nodded. "It's not something to be accepted lightly," Sarah warned. "It will be a lot of work. But if you do well at the exhibition it could make your career. I want you to think about it for a couple of days and make sure you can commit."

"I will. Thank you. I really appreciate this." Alice wanted to say yes straight away, but she knew Sarah would not accept that. She decided to take Sarah's advice and give it some serious thought; however, she couldn't help being excited. She couldn't wait to tell Ben about it. It was nearly lunchtime and she had arranged to meet Maya at the theatre. She was working on an enormous canvas creating the main backdrop for their production. It was a challenging project, but she was having a lot of fun. It was slower work than she had expected due to the sheer size of the piece. She either had to lay the canvas out on the floor of a hall or sports centre or she had to work on a scaffolding tower. She was not a huge fan of heights, but working that way had the advantage of keeping her in the theatre. It was the day of the dress rehearsal and while she was waiting for Maya, she sat in the front row to watch the cast rehearsing. She especially enjoyed watching Maya on the stage. She had a voice that made everyone stop and listen. Alice was mesmerized by her.

The two of them had become very close over the past few months, and Alice now thought of Maya almost as a sister. Their relationship was something of a mystery to the other students, who tended to keep a wide berth. Maya was loud and brash, bordering on rude. Many people didn't see what shy, quiet Alice could see in her. Alice felt like she was the only person in the world who knew Maya and could see her for the sweet and caring soul that she was. She knew that Maya had a sting in her tail, she had certainly seen her use it on other students, but she was always kind enough to Alice.

When they finally broke for lunch, Alice told Maya about the conversation she had just had with her tutor. "That's great. You are going to do it aren't you? You are an amazing artist." Maya said, unpeeling her banana and eating half of it in one mouthful. "Fuck, I'm starving. I thought that rehearsal was never going to end. That silly bitch playing Mother Superior kept fucking up. Did you see?" Alice frowned a little and pursed her lips, thinking about whether she should say something or not. She was worried about her friend. Maya had managed to alienate almost everyone else on her course and in the show. She had gone off the rails in the past couple of months and seemed to upset everyone she spoke to. Alice decided she had to say something. Even if it meant she would open herself up to Maya's wrath.

"Maya, I'm worried about you," Alice said, cautiously. She was trying to read Maya's face, but she was a closed book. "You were late again for rehearsal, and you have fallen out with everyone," she continued. "People are calling you names and trying to avoid you…" Maya shrugged her shoulders and looked down at her food. Alice could tell she was getting annoyed, but she knew she may not get another chance to broach the subject again. "You're angry all the time Maya. Every little thing sets you off. You may not realise how much you have changed, but honestly you are almost permanently on edge. What happened to you?" Maya flashed an angry look toward Alice. "Nothing happened. I'm just in a mood. It'll pass," she said with a dismissive shrug. "Maya," Alice persevered. "Only yesterday you screamed at one of the chorus members singing a bum note. The poor girl left in tears and hasn't come back."

"It's not my fault she's a shit singer. We are better off without her." Maya said around a mouthful of sandwich. "She's gonna have to grow a thicker skin if she wants to get on in this business. I was just giving her some constructive criticism."

"It's not really constructive to make people run away crying," Alice sighed. She wasn't going to get through. She usually tried to avoid all subjects that could cause an argument. By nature, she was a people pleaser and was comfortable in that role, but she could see Maya's behaviour becoming more self-destructive, so she made up her mind to invite her round for a girl's night. Maybe after a few drinks they would both be a bit more relaxed and she would be able to get Maya to confide in her. Ben was going to be out of town for the weekend at a conference, so the timing was perfect.

The alarm went off at eight that Saturday morning, but Alice couldn't drag herself out of bed. She hadn't gone to sleep particularly late, and she had slept well, having had the bed to herself. She felt lethargic, her arms and legs seemed to weigh ten times more than usual. She pressed snooze on the alarm and allowed herself another twenty minutes to doze. She must have fallen straight back into a deep sleep as the alarm woke her once again. This time she forced herself to get up. She had a long list of things to do and wanted to be ready to spend time with Maya that evening. Alice sat up and swung her legs around to sit on the edge of the bed, causing her stomach to flip, sending bile into her mouth. She half ran to the bathroom, barely making it to the toilet before throwing up. She sat down heavily on the floor, leaning her head against the cool metal of the radiator. Out of the corner of her eye she spotted the box of tampons that she had not had to use for quite some time. She began to sweat, her heart racing. How long had it been since she had had a period? She had always been irregular, but she should have come on by now surely. She got up from the floor, washed her face and brushed her teeth. In the bedroom she pulled up the calendar on her phone. She was late. She couldn't understand it, she had been so careful. Nausea threatened to overwhelm her again, so she took a couple of deep breaths to calm herself down.

An hour later Alice was in the supermarket buying pizza and ice cream for her evening with Maya. She wandered up and down the wine aisle several times trying to choose a bottle but found that the mere thought of drinking it made her feel nauseous again. She picked up a bottle of Chardonnay for Maya and some carbonated water for her. She forced herself to go to the medical aisle to pick up a pregnancy test. There were several brands to choose from, and she was not sure which was good, so she picked up one of each and hurried over to the self-checkout to pay.

Maya knocked on the door at six that evening. She was almost an hour early, sending Alice into a tailspin. She was not ready for her yet. She had planned to take the test and clean the bathroom before her guest had arrived, but all afternoon she had been putting it off. Too late now. She shoved the tests into the bathroom cabinet and headed to the door to let her friend in. Maya was knocking repeatedly on the door, becoming more and more impatient.

"Alright" shouted Alice "I'm coming already" She opened the door and before she had a chance to say anything Maya was in, pacing up and down the short hallway.

"About fucking time Alice, I'm freaking out here" Maya strode into the kitchen and filled a glass of water from the tap. Alice followed her and joined her on the window seat. "Whatever it is Maya, you need to calm down. Take a breath. Do you want to talk about it?"

"Yes, I want to talk about it. But you have got to promise you won't tell my mum. I don't need her giving me any shit right now." Maya began pacing again. Before giving Alice a chance to respond she said "I'm pregnant. Oh fuck, it sounds worse when I say it out loud. I'm pregnant and I have no partner and I have just been accepted to drama school, and basically everything is fucked." She sat back down next to Alice who put her arm around her shoulder and let her sob. A few minutes passed this way with both lost in their own thoughts.

"You are not alone" said Alice, quietly. "Yeah thanks" Said Maya. "No, I mean you are really not alone. I'm pregnant too," Alice continued. Maya stopped crying and looked her friend in the face. "You too. Really?" Said Maya. "Does Ben know?"

Alice laughed "Not yet. I don't even know yet. Well not really. I need to do a test. I was going to do it before you came, but you got here early."

"Well, do it now" said Maya. "You go and do the test and I will make us a cup of tea."

Ten minutes later Maya was sat at the table with tea and cake. Alice walked in holding the positive test in front of her. "So," said Maya, "How far along are you?" Alice looked on her phone again, checking the calendar to try to work it out. "Hmm, Anywhere between eight to sixteen weeks. I need to make a GP appointment. How about you?" "Only just six weeks. I am regular as clockwork usually, so I took a test as soon as I was late," said Maya. "so, that's my future down the toilet." She shook her head and sighed, trying hard not to burst into tears again.

"Your life is not over" said Alice, "You have options, there are always options". Maya shook her head. "I can't get an abortion if that's what you mean. No way."

"Ok," said Alice, "Well Ben and I are here for you. And your baby will have a playmate" she smiled, rubbing her stomach. "How about the father? Will he help? I didn't even know you were dating anyone."

"No. I can't tell him. It's too complicated. And I'm not dating anyone." Maya filled the kettle again and cut herself another slice of cake. "What's my mum going to say? She worked as hard as me to get a place at drama school. She will be gutted". Alice reached across the table to hold Maya's hand. "She will come round to the idea," Alice said, smiling. "She is going to be a Grandma after all". Maya thought about it for a second. "You're right, fuck it, let's do this!" She picked up her mobile from the table and walked into the lounge for a bit of privacy. Alice decided to follow her friend's example. She should tell Ben, and there was no time like the present. He had told her several times that he wanted to have kids, so she was sure he was going to be pleased. The phone went to voicemail, so she hung up without saying anything. This was not something she could say in a voice message. It would wait.

"Well, that could have gone better" said Maya as she came back into the room. "I'm a disappointment apparently." She flopped back down onto the window seat. "What else is there to eat? Pregnancy makes me hungry."

Alice got up to put the pizza in the oven. "Don't worry about your Mum. She will come round when she has had a chance to get used to the idea. Maybe she will love being a Grandma." Maya grunted in reply. "And," continued Alice, "there's no reason why you can't go back to school once you have had the baby. This really doesn't have to be a big disaster." She rubbed Maya's shoulder, trying to cheer her up. "Oh really," said Maya, a grim look on her face. "Are you going to be able to enter the exhibition now if you are due to drop a sprog when it opens? Seems like that might be a disaster."

Alice removed her hand from Maya's shoulder and wrapped her arms around herself. "Oh my god. The exhibition. I had forgotten about that." Alice sat down hard on the sofa next to Maya and sighed. "Oh well, not much I can do about that now. Got to look on the bright side. Having a baby could be kind of wonderful." She smiled and leaned her head on Maya's shoulder. "Yes. I think you might be right." Maya agreed. The two women enjoyed the rest of the evening. They polished off the pizza and watched films on Netflix until late. It was too late for Maya to go home, so Alice made up the bed for her in the spare room. She had not managed to get hold of Ben all evening, and she was starting to worry. It was gone two am, and he would probably be sleeping, but Alice didn't want to wait. She decided to video chat him, she wanted to see his face when she told him he was going to be a Dad. He picked up after a couple of rings, but he obviously had just accepted the call without looking as she was staring at an image of his ear. The lights were on in his room, so Alice was confident she had not woken him. He slurred a little when he said Hello, so she guessed he must have been drinking with the other conference delegates. "Ben, it's a video chat. I'm looking at your ear" She laughed. She watched the screen as Ben appeared. He looked worried, guilty even, and she immediately knew something was wrong. "Hold on a minute" he said. The screen went blank for a second, his hand was across the camera. When he appeared again, he was in the bathroom. "What's going on Ben?" she asked. "Is something wrong? Are you hiding something?" Ben's face darkened, his expression angry. "I should be asking you what's wrong. Why are you calling me in the middle of the night?" he almost shouted down the phone at her. "Couldn't it wait? I am working here Alice. You know that."

Alice took a deep breath to steady herself. "Yes Ben, it can wait." She shut down the call and angrily flicked off the light. She laid back on the pillow but couldn't close her eyes to sleep. She was too upset. Why was he awake at that time of night? Why didn't he want to talk to her? And why did he cover the camera? Alice was scared that she knew the answer to those questions, but she didn't want to admit it to herself. Not now. Everything had been going so well for them. This should have been the icing on the cake. What would she do if she were left to raise a baby alone? Suddenly she could sympathise with Maya and her situation.

Alice couldn't sleep. Her mind would not stop spinning long enough to let her drop off, so she got up as the sun started to rise and made herself a cup of coffee. She took it back to the bedroom, making sure not to wake Maya up, and drank it sitting up in bed. She must have dozed for a short time as she was woken by the phone ringing. It was Ben. He looked tired but he was smiling. She knew this face. This was the face he used when he wanted to charm her. "I'm sorry about last night, babe" he started. "How are you?" Alice was still angry with him, but she kept her feelings in check. They were going to be a family, and that was more important than a stupid fight. She was probably over-reacting. He was just drunk. They could talk about that another day. This should be a happy time for both of them. "I'm fine" she said, unable to hide her smile. "In fact, I'm better than fine. You are going to be a Dad." Ben's face split into a huge grin. "That's fantastic news," he let out a whoop of joy. "I should be there with you. I'm coming home" He said, decisively. Alice laughed, relieved that he was excited about it. "I'm fine. I have Maya here. You finish your conference and I will see you tomorrow evening. We can celebrate then." Ben agreed, and when they ended the call Alice let out a sigh. She had been silly to doubt him. Ben loved her, and he was going to be a great Dad.

Alice quickly fell back to sleep, her mind clear now that she had spoken to Ben. She was woken at ten by Maya knocking gently on her bedroom door. "I brought you coffee" she said, slipping into the room. "I'm just about to have breakfast. Do you want something?" Alice sat up and checked her watch. "How about we go out for breakfast, then we can do some baby shopping. We have the whole day" Alice was in too good a mood to waste sitting indoors. She wanted to spend the day looking at baby clothes and buying teddy bears with her best friend. She didn't want to worry about her course or her relationship or the exhibition right now. That could all wait until Monday. For now, she just wanted to enjoy her pregnancy before the rest of her life could get in the way.

CHAPTER 16
MAGGIE 2012

Maggie pulled her black, woollen coat tightly around her as she stepped out of the limousine at the chapel in her parent's hometown. She had been dreading this moment the whole week, playing scenarios over and over in her mind. Now she was here it was even worse that she expected. Daniel appeared beside her with an umbrella and took her arm to lead her toward the chapel of rest. He had been hovering around her all week, asking how she was and bringing her endless cups of tea which were left to go cold and undrunk. She knew he was concerned about her, but his constant attention was getting on her nerves. She could see some of her parent's friends and their few remaining family members all huddled together under an overhang that created a meagre shelter from the weather. She couldn't face speaking to any of them right now.

Daniel had his arm around her and was holding the umbrella in the other hand to shelter them from the worst of the weather. She turned her face into his body and allowed him to steer her away from the gaggle of relatives, toward the chapel entrance. The usher at the door was sympathetic and pulled back the heavy drapes across the door to allow them to slip quietly inside. The room was filled with a thousand flowers and the scent of jasmine was thick, making Maggie feel slightly dizzy and faint. She sat heavily on the pew at the front of the room and waited in place for the coffins to be brought in and for all the other mourners to join her. She became aware of the dead weight of Daniels arm pressing down on her shoulders, making her feel claustrophobic, and shrugged him off to take a deep breath. She had a sudden urge to run, and glanced reflexively round the room, checking her exits. She caught a glimpse of Daniel's worried frown out of the corner of her eye and patted his hand on his knee to reassure him. She had known him since they first started secondary school fourteen years ago, when she had intervened as a bully tried to steal his lunch money. She had always been the strong one, the protector, and she knew it worried him deeply when she was struggling emotionally. He tried desperately to help her, but Maggie was always aware that underneath the brave face he was holding on with fingertips to stop himself succumbing to panic. She managed to throw him a small smile as the strains of "In the Arms of the Angel" began to play and the caskets were brought in and placed on stands in front of them.

The funeral service passed in a blur. Maggie felt as though she was watching it through someone else's eyes, somehow removed from it, as though it were happening to someone else altogether. She was barely aware of what was being said. She was watching a small butterfly that had somehow found itself in the building and was flying in seemingly pointless circles in the air above the altar. Speakers came and went without her retaining anything they had said. In the car on the way to the wake after the service, she turned to Daniel and spoke to him for the first time that day. "I want to be a foster mum. My parents gave me a whole life of wonderful memories. I can't repay them for that, but I can do the same for another child. We can. Together. Let's foster a child. What do you think?" She looked up at Daniel with tears in her eyes. His initial surprise quickly gave way to a smile. "Yes. Let's do it," he said, making a decision in a split second. He hugged her tightly. "Let's be parents." Maggie hugged him back and laid her head on his shoulder, allowing the tears she had held on to all morning to slip down her cheeks. Daniel was her soulmate and the other half of her. She had known that from the moment she had met him. He was the first person she wanted to tell when something good happened and was the only person who she trusted with her deepest secrets. She couldn't think of a more perfect way to share him with the world than to be by his side as they shared their love and their home with a child. They had talked many times about having a child of their own one day, but something had always held Maggie back. She had been fostered by her parents as a baby and they had adopted her when she was three years old. They were the only parents she had ever known, and they had meant the world to her. Her father had been the headmaster of a school for boys with learning disabilities, and her mum had stayed at home to look after Maggie and the house. She was a creative woman and had made her mark all around the home. There was not a handicraft she couldn't turn her hand to, and in every room, there were elements that she had made, from curtains and cushions in the lounge, to handmade soaps and candles in the bathroom. Every room held reminders of her.

The wake was being held in Maggie's childhood home. It was a large, detached house with a wrap-around garden that contained her childhood tree house and swing set. There were four large bedrooms and an extension downstairs that created a large open plan kitchen/diner with folding doors that led to a raised decking area. It was an unseasonably warm spring day, so the doors had been opened to allow guests to use the garden to make more space. Maggie had called in caterers and instructed them to provide a buffet for fifty people, but she was starting to worry that she had not provided enough food. Her parents had obviously been well liked in the neighbourhood, as dozens of people had arrived to pay their respects. The house and garden were full of people who all had happy stories to tell of her parents. She spent a couple of hours moving from group to group, receiving condolences and listening to expressions of sorrow and love, before retiring to her old bedroom for a bit of quiet and privacy. She lay back on the bed and breathed in the scent of her mother's favourite washing powder. She hadn't slept in that bed for years, but her mum had still laundered the bedclothes every week, just in case. The smell brought back memories of bedtimes stories, sleepovers, and late-night exam revision. She closed her eyes and allowed herself to drift off to sleep.

The light was starting to fade when she awoke an hour or more later. Daniel had crept into the room and spooned up next to her at some point. "Everyone's gone" he said, stroking her hair. She breathed a sigh of relief. She couldn't face anyone again right now. The stress of the past few weeks was starting to sink in and every muscle in her body ached with exhaustion. She rolled over to face Daniel and allowed him to kiss her on the forehead. "What do you think about moving here, keeping the house? I would love to raise our kids here." She could just make out Daniels face in the twilight, the light from the streetlamp was reflected in his eye. "Sounds perfect." He kissed her, on the mouth this time, and wrapped his arms around her.

CHAPTER 17
ALICE 2019

Alice laid as still as she could in the bed carefully controlling her breathing. She had been listening to Ben snoring on his side of the bed for the past ten minutes and was trying to gather the nerve to get up. As carefully as she could she swung her legs over the side of the bed and sat up. A sharp pain in her side caused her to let out a cry, which she muffled with her hand. She froze in place and checked to see if Ben had woken. Satisfied he was still sleeping she headed toward the door. The floor was covered in shards of glass, from the broken mirror, so she had to tread carefully as she tip-toed to the door. There was a full moon that shone through the open curtains and reflected in the mirror shards, illuminating the room enough for her to be able to see.

Once she was in the hall Alice hurried along to Lottie's bedroom and scooped the little girl up in her arms. She had always been a good sleeper and didn't even wake as Alice wrapped a blanket around her and carried her down the stairs to strap her into the double buggy. Alice left Lottie in the lounge, pulling the door to, and headed to the kitchen where she made up a bottle of milk for Alfie and threw some formula and spare nappies into a carrier bag. She grabbed her handbag and mobile phone and stowed them under the buggy. Taking the warm bottle of milk, Alice crept quietly back up the stairs and slipped into the nursery. With as little noise as possible, Alice picked up Alfie, who was warm and comfortable in his baby sleeping bag and slipped the teat into his mouth. He sucked happily on the warm milk without making a fuss, so Alice carried him downstairs and carefully strapped him in beside his sister in the buggy.

Alice could see out of the glass in the front door that there was already a heavy frost on the ground. She was wearing just a pair of pyjama shorts and a vest top. She would freeze to death if she went out dressed like that. All her shoes were upstairs in the bedroom closet, so she would have to go without them. Her winter coat hung on a peg beside the door, so she slipped that around her bare shoulders and wrapped a scarf around her neck. She took Ben's ski jacket and tucked it around the two sleeping children. Still making sure to make no noise, Alice opened the front door and manoeuvred the buggy out into the night. A blast of icy air forced the door open wide, but she managed to catch the edge of it before it slammed into the wall. Ben moved upstairs, but the snoring resumed, so she pulled the door closed behind her.

The buggy was unwieldy with the bags and coat hanging from it, and Alice was numb with the cold. She didn't know what time it was, but the streetlights had gone off, so she guessed it was around 3am. Her feet were stinging with the brutal cold, and she knew she would get hypothermia if she stayed outside too long, She half walked, half jogged as fast as her aching legs would allow her past the town centre and out to the riverside and the safety of Maggie's flat. Ben didn't know where Maggie lived, so the three of them should be safe there until she could make a plan.

Alice was shaking violently by the time she reached the stairs to the flat. There was no way she could carry the buggy up the stairs in this state, and she didn't want to wake the children and scare them. Her phone was out of battery so she couldn't call anyone, so Alice was forced to leave her sleeping babies on the pavement and run up the stairs to wake Maggie to help her with them. "I'm sorry babies, Mummy's sorry," she sobbed as she tucked them in the shadows against the side of the building and ran as fast as she could up the stairs. She knocked on Maggie's door, quietly at first, as she didn't want to wake the neighbours. Alice couldn't hear a sound from inside the flat, and by now was beginning to panic, so she knocked harder and harder still on the door until she was bashing on the doorbell with all her might and screaming "let me in , let me in , let me in" at the top of her voice. A frightened looking Maggie opened the door and taking once look at the shaken and blue Alice, guided her inside. "The children are downstairs" screamed Alice, who set off at a run down the stairs to collect them. Maggie followed and helped Alice carry the buggy up the stairs. Miraculously Alfie had not woken throughout the ordeal and Lottie was sleepy enough that she was content to sit quietly and watch what was going on. Once they were inside the flat Maggie busied herself carrying the children into her room and tucking them in to her warm double bed. Alice was pleased that Maggie had taken control of the situation as once they were in and the door was safely closed behind them, the enormity of what Alice had done hit her and she began shaking once again. Maggie handed her a dressing gown and helped her into it, wrapping it tightly around her to warm her. The adrenaline that had fuelled her up to now was starting to leave her body and she noticed how cold she was. She slipped her legs under the duvet and rested her back against the headboard. Maggie had barely said a word and Alice was thankful for that. She didn't think she could speak right now even if she wanted to. Lottie had drifted back off to sleep snuggled up close to her brother. Alice stroked their hair and sobbed quietly into the collar of the dressing gown. Maggie appeared again in the bedroom doorway with a steaming cup of tea which she placed in Alice's hands. She wrapped her fingers around the cup, warming them through.

"Is there anyone you want me to call?" said Maggie quietly, taking a seat on the end of the bed. Alice shook her head. She couldn't think of anyone who would be able to help her. She and the children were safe, that's all she needed for now. She didn't have room for anything else in her brain. "Is the door shut?" She asked Maggie. "Can you check it?" Maggie said that she would and left to do as she was asked. Alice heard her test the door handle and rattle the lock, then return to the room. "do you think we could put something up against it?" she asked Maggie. Afraid that she would say no or laugh at her. Without showing any hint of surprise Maggie replied "Sure. No problem" and left the room again. This time Alice could hear her slide the heavy sideboard across the room. Alice slid out of bed to take a look at the fortified defences. Maggie had pulled the heavy curtain across the two glass viewing panels either side of the door and pushed the sideboard across the opening. She had then pushed the armchair up against that. Satisfied, Alice walked carefully back to the bedroom. She was still shaking violently, though whether that was from cold or fear, she couldn't tell. She felt exhausted all of a sudden, as though every part of her body were an impossibly heavy weight. She slid back into bed with the children without removing the dressing gown and pulled the duvet up tightly around her neck. She was vaguely aware of Maggie dimming the lights and leaving the room before she fell into a deep sleep.

Alice didn't know how long she had been asleep when she was woken by Maggie shaking her shoulder gently in the dimly lit room. "Bens here" Maggie said, putting her finger to her lips to shush her. Alice sat up with a start, reflexively pulling the neck of the dressing gown tightly closed. She moved over to allow Maggie to slide into the bed next to her and they sat silently listening to him banging on the door.

"I know she's in there with you. Open the fucking door. Alice, give me my fucking kids back, you fucking bitch. I know you're in there" Ben alternately shouted and banged heavily on the door. He was slurring his words badly and could only barely be understood, though his intent was quite clear. "Open the fucking door you slut. I need to talk to my wife"

"What do you want me to do?" Maggie whispered to Alice in the bedroom. "Shall I call the police?"

"No, don't do that" Alice replied swiftly. "It will only make things worse. Most of the police in this town are his mates." Maggie nodded; her brow creased. There was a small spot of blood on her bottom lip where she had been biting it. Alice wondered if Maggie would call the police anyway if Ben carried on, regardless of what she wanted her to do.

"It's gone quiet" Said Maggie. "I think he left. He doesn't know you are here. He's just trying his luck." The two of them sat stock still for a couple of minutes, straining to hear any noises from the entrance hall. After a few minutes of silence Maggie decided to be brave and peer through one of the side viewing windows. She crept across the room and stealthily drew back the corner of the velvet curtain. She was confronted with a close-up of Ben's eye against the glass. He saw her and started banging and screaming once again. "I can see you in there. Let me in. Let me see my wife." Without a word Maggie closed the curtain and walked away. Looking around, she realized that the buggy was just about visible to him through the gap in the curtain. She was sure he would have spotted it.

Maggie joined Alice back in the bedroom, closing the door firmly behind her. Both the children had been woken by the noise outside. Lottie was clinging to her mum, sobbing loudly. Alice was shaking again, but she was managing to control her emotions in front of the children. "It's okay baby" she said to Lottie as she wiped tears from her rosy cheeks "Daddy is being silly, so we are having a sleepover with Aunty Maggie, Ok?" Lottie nodded her head, her blonde curls bouncing on the back of her neck. Maggie sat back on the bed and tickled Lottie under the chin making her squirm and giggle. "You are such a brave girl," she told her. "How about you watch some cartoons on my Ipad while I talk to Mummy?" Lottie nodded, a smile creeping to the edges of her mouth. Maggie gave her the tablet and moved away to talk to Alice. Ben could still be heard banging and swearing in the hallway along with the sound of movement from the flat below. He was obviously waking the neighbours now. "Alice, I think we need to call the police." She picked up her mobile phone from the night table where it was charging. "You don't have to tell them everything if you don't want to, but we just need to get him moved away from here for now." Alice nodded. She knew Maggie was right, but she couldn't bring herself to do it. "Will you call them please?" she said, pushing the phone back toward Maggie. "If he gets in here, he will kill me. Make sure they know he can't come in here." Maggie nodded. "Of course I will. Don't worry. You are safe." Alice returned to the bed where Lottie and Alfie were now engrossed in Peppa Pig cartoons. She stroked their baby-soft hair, tears running freely down her face. How could she ever feel safe again?

CHAPTER 18
MAGGIE 2017

"I feel sick." Maggie said to Daniel for probably the fifth time that morning. "I don't know if I am excited or nervous." She was pacing up and down the living room, stopping halfway every few passes to peer out of the front window. "Why don't you sit down?" said Daniel, patting the seat of the couch next to him. "You are going to be exhausted before they even arrive." Maggie sighed and flopped down beside him. "What if they hate us? What if we screw them up and they end up in therapy for the rest of their lives because of us?" Daniel smoothed his hand up and down her back, trying to calm her. "Relax. You are going to be a great mother. And I know that because you are already worrying about their future. And if they do grow up to hate us, we will deal with it then." Maggie looked at him for a few seconds, weighing his words, before jumping up and resuming her pacing. "I don't know how you can just sit there all calm. Where are they? They should have been here half an hour ago." Daniel's reply was drowned out by a little yelp from Maggie. "Oh my god, they're here." She turned to face him, still as a statue, her face suddenly white. Daniel wondering if she was going to be sick picked up the waste-paper basket just in case. The doorbell rang and Maggie shook her head as if surfacing from a dive underwater. "Here we go," she said, taking Daniel's hand so they could open the front door side by side.

*

All Maggie and Daniel's time and energy over the past ten

months had been focussed on preparing to be parents. The process of fostering children had not been as difficult as Maggie had expected, but it had been long-winded and tiring. After losing her parents she had taken a year-long sabbatical from her job as a primary school teacher. Daniel ran his own web-based business at home, so they had had a lot of time together. They had moved into her childhood home and thrown themselves into the process of training to be foster parents. They had both excelled at the training courses. In fact they enjoyed meeting other couples who were planning to embark on the journey along with them, and they hoped to make friends who would form a support network along the way.

They decided early on that they would like to take in sibling groups as so often children were separated and placed in homes far apart from one another, which must be horrible for them. Maggie's heart broke to read all the awful stories about things that the children had all had to endure so early on in their young lives. She could barely stand it. She was pleased to find a small group of siblings after only a few days of looking and expressed an interest in meeting them as soon as possible.

Only days after they received word from the panel that they had been approved as foster parents, they were introduced to their chosen children, one girl, Soraya aged 7 and twin three-year-old boys Alex and Kenzi. They were born to an Algerian woman who had been making a living in the sex industry. She didn't have any family in England, so when she got involved heavily with drug use the children were taken away from her. She was now pregnant with a baby whose paternity was in doubt, and who was likely to be removed to a foster home and adopted as soon as he or she was born.

Daniel had been delighted when he found out the children were of mixed-race heritage, being black himself he had hoped to be lucky enough to foster children of colour. He wanted to be the role model they had been lacking in their life, as well as having a family that looked as though they belonged together. The past three days had been a whirlwind. Maggie and Daniel had met with social workers several times to hear the full history of the children. They had also had meetings with them at their current foster home every day. The children were outgoing and quick to trust, which Maggie thought was amazing considering their background story. Maggie had fallen in love with the children at first sight. She thought back to that first day.

Maggie and Daniel had held hands as they were invited into a big lounge, where the children were playing. The twins were building towers out of Lego and didn't say a word as Daniel sat down beside them and asked if he could join in. Alex shuffled over a little to make space for him to sit down before going back to what he was doing. Soraya had watched Maggie thoughtfully from the moment they entered over the top of her book. Her deep brown eyes glued to her every movement. Maggie sat on a sofa a small distance from the girl, not wanting to invade her space. "Hi, I'm Maggie," she said with a smile. "What are you reading?" Soraya lifted up the book to show Maggie the cover. "It's Harry Potter," she said. Her face impassive. She carefully placed a bookmark between the pages and set the book down on the table beside her. Maggie raised her eyebrows. "Wow, you must be a very good reader." Soraya nodded solemnly. Maggie glanced around the room, noticing some pencils and paper laid out on the coffee table. "Do you like to draw?" she asked. Soraya shrugged her shoulders. "I guess so." Maggie slid down off the seat, onto the floor beside the coffee table, picked up a pencil and began drawing. She was acutely aware of the social worker and carers watching her from the door but did her best to appear at ease so she didn't spook Soraya. Maggie was pleased when Soraya sat down on the floor next to her and pulled a piece of paper toward her. "What are you drawing?" she asked, peering at Maggie's page. "It's supposed to be an owl. I was trying to draw Hedwig for you," she said, adding a background to her picture. Soraya looked at it appraisingly. "It's not very good is it?"

she stated, matter of fact. "Hedwig doesn't wear boots." She turned her head to the side, looking at the picture from all angles. "Those aren't boots." Maggie replied. "She is carrying a letter in her claws." Soraya looked at the picture again and nodded, before picking up a pencil and making a start on her own drawing. "They are called talons on an owl," she said without looking up. "Not claws. They are talons. Owls are predators. They catch their prey in their talons. Owls are nocturnal raptors." Maggie was impressed. "You know a lot about owls huh?" Soraya shrugged again. "I like reading. It was in one of my books." She went back to her drawing, which Maggie could see was taking the shape of some sort of dragon. "You know Soraya, I'm a schoolteacher and I wish some of my students liked reading like you do." Soraya put down her pencil and turned toward Maggie. "Is there a library at your school?" she asked, interest sparkling in her eyes. Maggie faced her and smiled. "Yes of course. Maybe you would like to come and see it one day?" Soraya's face lit up for a second with excitement before she caught hold of it and resumed her neutral expression once again. "Maybe." Maggie went back to her drawing. The short exchange made her sad. Soraya obviously loved books but didn't want to show anyone that she was excited about visiting the library. No child should have to keep such a tight control over their emotions. Maybe she didn't want to get her hopes up. She must have experienced a lot of disappointment in her short life. Soraya was still watching her. Maggie got the feeling that she was being evaluated. She coloured in her picture for a minute, giving Soraya time to come to her. She was still acutely aware of being observed and hoped that the social worker didn't think she was just ignoring the girl. After another minute Soraya spoke quietly, without looking up from her drawing. "My social worker said you are going to be our new carers."

"Yes, we hope to be," said Maggie, "If that's ok with you?" Soraya carried on drawing. "Do you have books at your house?"

"Yes, we have lots of books. And if there is a book you particularly want, we could go out and get if for you." Soraya nodded thoughtfully to herself. "And what about strawberry milk?" she asked. "Alex and Kenzi like strawberry milk."

"We could definitely get strawberry milk. I can't see a problem with that," said Maggie. She put the pencil she was using down on the table and sat back, resting her back against the sofa. Soraya followed her lead, sitting cross-legged facing Maggie. The girl looked around the room, taking note of Daniel playing with the twins, who were giggling as he pretended to be Godzilla smashing up a city full of Lego buildings. "Are we allowed to call you Mummy and Daddy?" Soraya asked. Her eyes full of hope. Maggie was flattered, she flicked a glance toward the social worker who gave a tiny nod of approval. "We would love for you to call us Mummy and Daddy." Maggie said, glad that she was managing to keep herself from crying. "You can call us whatever you want to. We just want you to be happy," she smiled. Soraya sidled closer and took Maggie's hand in hers, practicing the sound of the word out loud several times, enjoying the feel of it on her lips. "Mummy, Mum, Mummy."

*

The two spare rooms of their new home had been transformed. Soraya's room was painted a fetching shade of lilac. Her duvet cover and curtains were adorned with unicorns and stars at the girl's request. Maggie had stocked the bookshelf with a range of age appropriate books and added a small desk area with notepads and pens in one corner. A large stuffed Hedwig toy sat in the prime spot on the pillows of the metal framed day bed. The boys would be sharing a room which had been painted in primary colours with a collage of Lego character stickers placed at strategic positions around the room. There were two matching beds, which could be made into bunk beds as the boys grew and needed more space, but for now they were side by side. A huge box of Lego awaited the boys. Daniel had gathered it from storage at a friend's house last night and couldn't wait to see their faces when they saw how much of it there was.

The first few days were a massive learning curve for the new family. Soraya was extremely protective of the twins and would not allow Maggie to do anything for them. She insisted on changing their nappies and reading to them when it was time for bed and was constantly reminding Maggie and Alex when they needed feeding or a nap. She was hyper vigilant with them, never letting them out of her sight. All three children had some developmental and emotional issues due to the neglect they had suffered, but the twins definitely had it worst. Their mother was addicted to drugs, so they had been born dependent on heroin and had to be weaned off of it in the hospital. They were still both wearing nappies despite being nearly four years old, but the social worker insisted that that was completely normal in these circumstances. The fourth day they were there Maggie decided to try a different tactic to allow Soraya to take a break from the stress of watching over her brothers. She arranged for Daniel to look after the boys while she took Soraya out for the day alone. Despite her initial reluctance Soraya agreed to go. Maggie planned a day in the city shopping for clothes, eating ice cream and visiting the cinema.

Soraya was quiet in the car on the way to the shopping centre, barely saying two words for the entire journey. Maggie began to worry that she was doing something wrong and was in half a mind to turn the car around and go back the way they had come, however when they arrived at the concrete parking structure Soraya became excited and talkative again. "Go to the top Mummy. I love to be up high" she giggled, winding down the window and leaning her head out. "Hands and head inside the car please Soraya" said Maggie in her best mum voice and was pleased when Soraya pulled herself back into the car and plopped down onto the seat. "I can smell doughnuts" She squealed with delight, and Maggie knew she had done the right thing.

The two of them shopped for a couple of happy hours. Soraya chose some denim dungarees and a trendy sweatshirt for herself, along with some converse trainers covered in purple sequins. Maggie teased her about how bling they were, while being secretly jealous of the little girls' choice of footwear. Maggie picked up a couple of sets of clothing for each of the boys and couldn't resist buying them both a toy truck with flashing lights and sounds. Soraya had never been shopping like this before and Maggie had to admit that she spent rather more on her than she had originally intended. Soraya had never had anything new for herself and the look of pure pleasure and excitement in her eyes when Maggie said she could choose a gift was a delight to see. Soraya chose a backpack for school and some fairy lights to put up in her room. After lunch at a pizza place, followed by huge ice creams sundaes, Maggie took her to watch the latest Disney offering at the big cinema complex on the edge of town. As the lights went down Soraya slipped her hand into Maggie's and gave it a squeeze. She leaned her head onto Maggie's arm and stayed that way for the majority of the film. When they returned home that evening the boys were already bathed and in their pyjamas. Soraya was so happy talking to Maggie all about her day that she forgot to worry about her brothers. That evening Daniel read them a story and put them to bed while Soraya happily drew pictures and chatted to Maggie in the lounge.

The boys were both very good sleepers, but Soraya regularly suffered from night terrors. On several occasions in the first few weeks with Maggie and Daniel, they were awoken to the sound of her running around the house screaming at the top of her voice. It was incredibly stressful to watch and Daniel especially found it distressing to see her obviously very frightened but beyond his help. Each time it happened they asked Soraya about it the next day, but she could never remember what she had dreamed about. Daniel called the social worker, who assured him that it was completely normal and would go away in time. Maggie and Daniel moved a spare mattress into Soraya's room and Maggie started sleeping in there with her to try to catch her before the dreams took hold. The tactic worked and within a couple of weeks Soraya was sleeping much better and the night terrors were reduced in frequency. However, Soraya was getting very attached to Maggie and was dependent on her being in the room with her when she fell asleep. Maggie was secretly flattered by it and her and Daniel agreed that in the short term it would not hurt for her to sleep in the same room as Soraya if it would make the child feel more confident. She had suffered so much in her short, little life, she deserved some comfort and safety.

Maggie was proud of how well Daniel had adapted to being a father. His devotion to the children was adorable. He loved every moment with them, never complaining about lack of sleep or having to tidy up after the children ten times a day. He even enjoyed potty training the twins, celebrating each time they managed to wee on the potty as if they had just won a talent contest. The boys were totally in love with him. He never tired of playing Lego with them, or chasing them round the park, pushing them on the swings or teaching them to ride their first trike. He was careful to always include Soraya in their games, but she was far happier to spend time with Maggie. She loved to help her in the kitchen and was a quick learner. Maggie took her grocery shopping and the two of them planned meals and picnics together. Soraya had a fantastic imagination and loved to write her stories down in her notebooks, illustrating them herself in her own creative style.

Toward the end of August Daniel and Maggie sat in the garden one warm evening once all the children were asleep. Daniel opened a bottle of wine, poured a glass for each of them then joined Maggie on the garden swing. Maggie took a large swig of the wine and smiled at Daniel.

"What's that face for?" he laughed. "Nothing. I'm just happy," she replied. He took her glass from her and placed it on the floor, leaning in to kiss her, his hands in her hair. "I'm happy too" he said. He picked the glass back up and handed it to her, leaning back on the swing. "I've been thinking about what happens at the start of term" he began. Maggie watched him out of the corner of her eye as he continued. "I think I'd like to take a sabbatical for a year and just spend some time with the kids" He looked at her with eyebrows raised in question. Maggie took another sip of her wine. She had been waiting for something like this. She had never seen Daniel so happy. Of course she thought it was a good idea. "Well?" he said, Impatient for an answer. "Oh, I didn't realise you were asking me" Maggie teased. She smiled broadly at him and Daniel relaxed a little on the seat. He had obviously worried about what she would say, though she couldn't for the life of her think why. "It's a great idea" She agreed. "take a year off to be a stay at home Dad. It will be good for all of us." Daniel flung his arms around her and hugged her tight, almost spilling her wine. "I love you Maggie Crossford" he said.

"I love you back" she laughed.

CHAPTER 19
MAGGIE 2019

"Morning," Maggie greeted Alice when she appeared in the kitchen, yawning extravagantly, and brushing her uncombed hair out of her eyes with her fingers. "Coffee?" she asked, pouring her a cup of rich, nutty liquid into a large mug and handing it to her. Alice took the cup with a lopsided grin and sat next to her daughter at the dining table, tucking one leg under herself. She pulled Lottie to her in order to kiss her curly hair, only to be waved away with a chubby little hand. "Busy Mummy. Painting" She said, turning back to the colouring book she was working on.

"I'm so sorry I slept in..." Alice began, before being hushed immediately by Maggie. "Nonsense. We have been having a lovely morning." She took a wet-wipe from a packet on the table and wiped the remnants of sticky oats from Alfie's chin. She handed him a piece of apple which he gnawed on contentedly while she gathered up dirty plates and cups and loaded the dishwasher. "I have enjoyed having children around again. And you obviously needed the sleep..." Maggie turned her back to Alice and busied herself at the sink, hoping that she had not noticed her slip up. Alice didn't know she had had children, and it wouldn't be good for either of them if that were to come up right now. She enjoyed living here and had not managed to do what she wanted to do yet. She made a note to herself to be more careful in future. Luckily, she seemed to have gotten away with it. Alice was engrossed with playing with Alfie. "So, I thought we could go and take a look at the tearoom today. I picked up the keys yesterday.

What do you think?"

"I don't know, I don't think I'm ready yet," Alice said. She fiddled with the cord of the dressing gown she was wearing, winding and unwinding it around her fingers. "It's just, you know, Ben knows everyone, and they will all be judging me, and..."

"It's ok" Maggie jumped in, holding her hands up to calm Alice down. "It's not a problem

. You just stay here as long as you need to." Alice's shoulders relaxed and she let the gown cord fall from her hands. "Why don't I take the Lottie out with me today to give you some time with Alfie?" Maggie suggested. She had been thinking about this all morning, and hoped it came across as spontaneous. "I could take her to playgroup then pop in to the tearoom to measure up on the way back" Lottie, who had been listening in to the conversation chimed up with a chorus of "playgroup, playgroup, playgroup" making both Maggie and Alice laugh.

"Well," Said Alice, "I guess that's settled. Come on Lottie, let's go and find you some clothes to wear" Maggie watched Lottie bounce out of the room with her Mum. She had been shopping the day before and bought clothes and shoes for all three of her new house guests. She had enjoyed wandering the supermarket aisles picking out outfits for the children. Alice had not yet worn anything other than the long-sleeved pyjamas and dressing gown that Maggie had given her, and she was starting to worry about her. She decided to allow Alice two more days to recover at home before she tried in earnest to get her to get dressed and leave the house.

Lottie skipped out of the bedroom a couple of minutes later, hair neatly combed and plaited, wearing a mermaid jumper and flashing trainers. Maggie helped her into her coat and mittens and the little girl slipped her hand into Maggie's, hurrying her toward the door. "Let's go say bye to Mummy" Maggie said as she popped her head around the door to the lounge. "are you sure you're ok?" she asked Alice one more time. "Do you need anything?"

"No thanks." Replied Alice. "We're fine. Make sure you lock the door on your way out." Maggie agreed and headed down the stairs with Lottie who insisted on jumping down each stair individually, squealing with joy each time it made the lights flash on the soles of her trainers. Maggie checked her watch. She was hoping to get to the library early so she could see Maya before the group started. She had missed her over the past few days and could barely contain her excitement at the thought of speaking to her again today. She had been trying to think of ways to engineer a meeting with her and had rehearsed several conversations over and over in her head. As it happened, she needn't have worried. Maya was waiting for her outside the library. She spotted her from almost two blocks away, her height and striking locks giving her away immediately. Maya spotted the two of them heading toward her and steered Freddie in his buggy down the pavement to meet them.

"Where's Alice?" Maya asked, terse to the point of rudeness. "Erm, hi," said Maggie. "Hello Freddie." She smiled at the little boy and nodded to Lottie who had asked if she could run in with him.

"Sorry, yeah. Hi," said Maya, quieter now. "Is Alice ok? Ben has been calling me all week, frantic. Poor bloke. Is she with you?" Maggie's eyebrows creased. "Poor Ben? Really?" She replied, without waiting for an answer. "Yes, she's with me. She's fine, by the way, not that you asked" Maggie strode away from Maya into the library to find Lottie and take their seats. Maya was close behind her, talking to the back of her retreating head. "Ben called me last night to say Alice had gone crazy on him, smashed up the house and took the kids while he was sleeping" She said, a little louder than necessary. Maggie stopped dead in her tracks and wheeled round abruptly to face Maya, who almost knocked her over with the momentum she had built up.

"What on earth do you mean *she* went crazy? Alice is not the bad guy in this story," she said, glaring at Maya, both arms crossed. "Have you seen the bruises and cuts all over Alice's body?" She asked Maya, at little more than a whisper, forcing the taller woman to sit down once again. If Maya had been about to respond it was cut short by the singing library assistant once again. It was not until the session ended that Maya managed to find her way to Maggie's side again. "I'm sorry about earlier" She said, in a voice that sounded not entirely sincere to Maggie. "I miss her. Can you tell me where she is? I'm worried." Maya said. She batted her huge puppy dog brown eyes and Maggie felt her insides turn to liquid as she turned away, buying some more time to decide what to say. "Alice is fine. She's safe. You can come and see for yourself if you want". Maggie said, rather spur of the moment. She hoped she had done the right thing and would not be upsetting Alice more that she already was. On the other hand, she didn't want to turn down another opportunity to have Maya in her house. "I am popping over to the old lifeboat station to do some more measuring up for the tearoom on the way back. I could use your help if you have some time?" Maggie asked.

Maya's face lit up. "Yeah, deffo up for that. Can't wait to see it." Maggie beamed back at her, excited by her enthusiasm. Not wanting to waste any time she called Lottie over from where she was playing with Freddie at the beading table in the corner. Lottie grabbed the boy's hand and led him back over to his pushchair, ready to go. Maggie felt a wave of affection for the two children. She wanted nothing more than to pick them both up and hug them to her chest.

On their way to the station, Maggie broached the subject of Alice with Maya. "What did you mean earlier when you said Alice went crazy?" She kept her tone light, as she didn't want Lottie to pick up on what they were talking about. Maya was quiet for almost a minute and Maggie watched her out of the corner of her eye. She wondered if Maya had not heard her, or if she was choosing to ignore the question.

"Look, I don't want to tell you what to think, but Alice has quite an imagination" Maya said with a sigh. "She makes stuff up sometimes for attention." Maggie creased her eyes and shot Maya a quick look, trying to work out if she believed what she was saying. "Ben has been a family friend for as long as I can remember" she continued "And he has never been anything other than gentle and kind. Everyone loves him." Maya stopped walking and turned to face Maggie as she spoke. "I love Alice as a friend, but she has a history of mental illness" She said the last at a whisper, nodding her head for emphasis. "Sorry, but I have to believe Ben". Maggie stood still for a second, weighing up what she had heard. On the one hand she was thrilled that Maya was confiding in her, but on the other hand, she couldn't deny what she had seen. Something awful had happened to Alice to make her run naked from her home in the middle of a winter's night. She had left with nothing, no phone, no money, no clothes even. Surely, she would only do that if she were desperate. But on the other hand, what if she had done it because she was crazy. Maybe Maya was right. Maggie had no proof that the cuts and bruises she saw had been done by Ben. Could they be a product of self-harm? Alice had not wanted to press charges and she had not made a statement to the police yet. Was that because Ben was innocent?

Maya and the children were halfway up the road by now, so Maggie did a little run to catch up with them. She fished in her bag for her keys as they approached the lifeboat station door. There was a brisk wind, which blew sand up from the river edge into tiny whirlwinds around their legs. Maggie pushed open the glass door, gathering the pile of letters and junk mail that had accumulated there since she last visited. Maggie had arranged for a student from the local University to design a contemporary layout to the building for her, that would make the best use of the sea views and the huge picture windows. She had a large tape measure in her bag that she had been carrying around with her for a couple of days in case she got a chance to come in and take the measurements she needed. Maya and the children were standing by the windows, cleaning circles of dirt off the panes of glass so they could see out. "Come and hold the other end of this tape" Maggie called to Maya. Between the two of them they drew a basic plan of the building and took measurements. The children chased each other around the room, their happy squeals echoing off the empty walls.

"You should get my Mum in here" said Maya. "She's a whizz with a sewing machine. Whip up some curtains and chair covers in no time" Maggie jumped at the chance. She had been trying to find a way to wrangle a meeting with Pamela since she had arrived in Littleton, and Maya had just handed the opportunity to her. "Good idea," She said, trying not to sound overly eager "could you mention it to her next time you see her do you think? Only if she won't mind though"

"Yep, will do" Said Maya in her usual brusque manner. "Right, if we are done here, we only have forty minutes to see Alice. Freddie has a check-up this afternoon, don't you Bud?" she said, scooping the boy off his feet and blowing a raspberry on his neck before setting him back down next to Lottie, who was laughing, her tinkling laugh filling the cold room. Maggie gathered up her tape measure and notepad, taking a few snaps of the room on her phone before ushering everyone out so she could lock the door behind them.

The children ran ahead up the stairs to Maggie's flat, but she held back to speak to Maya. "Please don't say anything to Alice about Ben," she started. "I'm trying to give her time to talk about it when she's ready". "Fine, whatever," replied Maya with a shrug. "It's their business. Not mine." Maggie needn't have worried. Alice was pleased to see Maya. The two of them chatted as though nothing were out of the ordinary. For a few minutes Maggie envied their relationship. They were totally comfortable with each other. She was envious of that. Maya stayed about twenty minutes before taking Freddie for his appointment. When she left, Alice seemed to be in much better spirits. She asked Maggie to watch the children while she went for a shower, which Maggie happily agreed to. She took the pad and pen with the measurements she had made, out of her bag and proceeded to call her designer friend and arranged to meet him at the Station early the next morning. A quick google search produced the name of a local building contractor who she also invited to the meeting. Satisfied that things were starting to move she sat down to compose an email to Pamela Young, inviting her to come and see the Station and to talk about curtains. If things went to plan, she would be within touching distance of Pamela by this time tomorrow. She had waited for this moment as long as she could remember.

CHAPTER 20
ALICE 2015

"Hurry up Alice, the taxi is here" Ben shouted from downstairs. Alice looked at herself in bathroom the mirror, attempting to coax her wayward hair into some sort of style. Giving up, she slicked on some lip gloss and ran down the stairs to join Ben. He was already holding the taxi door open for her. As she stooped to get in, he whispered, "Your tits look amazing in that dress," and slid his hand onto her bum. She laughed and swatted his hand away. "Get in the car Moretti, you are making us late." He shut the door and shook his head as he jogged round to the other door. "Oh, the irony" he smiled. Alice settled back into the seat and clipped on her belt. She was regretting having agreed to go to Ben's office New Year's Eve party, but she decided to make the most of it for his sake. He seemed keen to go. His boss had booked a conference room in one of the best hotels in the area and had arranged a James Bond themed Casino Night with three course dinner and a free bar. Alice had been feeling sick all day, and the thought of drinking turned her stomach, but she had never been to a casino, and thought it might be fun.

Ben took her hand and kissed it, holding it to his face. "Thanks for doing this babe. I know it's not really your thing. Everyone will love you, I promise," he said. Alice wondered if he had already started on the champagne. She had to admit he did look pretty good tonight. He was wearing a black tuxedo complete with black bow tie, which perfectly complimented his olive complexion. He would give any James Bond actor a run for his money.

As soon as they walked into the hotel Ben was surrounded by people. The conference room was crowded. Most people had taken their seats at their allocated tables, but there were still dozens of people standing in groups chatting. Ben grabbed two glasses of champagne from a circulating waiter and handed her one. She took it from him, but the smell turned her stomach, so she put it back on the tray as the waiter circled round. They found their table and took a seat just as the starters were being brought out. Ben was sat to her left and was chatting to three women who were seated next to him. On her right was another group of women who were talking among themselves and made no attempt to include her in the conversation. Looking around the room Alice was surprised to see that the women outnumbered the men by a ratio of two to one. Usually at business functions it was the other way around. She busied herself by pouring a glass of water from the bottle on the table and fiddled with the cutlery until they were served with the first course of food for the evening.

Finally, Ben was released from his conversation with his colleagues and he turned to give her some attention. "Sorry about that," he began "Work talk, totally boring." Alice wanted to disagree. He had certainly seemed to find the conversation pretty engaging, but she was just being petty. "Don't worry about me" She told him. "I'm fine. You have as many work conversations as you want." Ben kissed her on the hand "You're the best" He said, raising an impatient hand to call the drinks waiter back over to him.

The second and third courses arrived with little change to the situation. Alice ate in silence, listening to what to her sounded like a rambling list of petty grievances and bitchy comments from Ben's friends, while he laughed and encouraged them to gossip and flirt with him. Alice couldn't bear gossips. Those nasty types who would make everyone's life a misery. There was one or two of them in every office, school and factory in the country, and Alice made it her policy to stay well away from them. She had met these two before, Trisha and Stacey. They were junior agents in the same office as Ben. They had all started around the same time. Ben had dated both of them before they met, but he assured her that there was nothing going on between them now. Alice was sure that was true as if they were still together, they would not be flirting so obviously with him now.

By 11pm Alice was ready for her bed. Ben was drunk by now and dancing wildly with everyone in the room. Alice was bored and tired. She decided Ben would not notice her leaving, so she took her bag and headed up to their room. She let herself in with the keycard and kicked off her shoes, sitting on the edge of the bed to rub her swollen ankles. As tired as she was Alice was not ready to go to sleep just yet. She made herself a hot chocolate using the coffee machine in the bedroom while running a hot bath using some lovely essential oils that had been provided by the hotel. She stepped into the bath enjoying the feeling of the warm water easing her aching muscles. From here she could hear the partyer's downstairs. The countdown to midnight was just beginning and she wondered what Ben would think when he noticed that she was not there. She wondered who he would kiss the new year in with. Stacey and Trisha were probably falling over themselves trying to be the closest to him when Big Ben chimed. The image that brought up in her mind made her smile. The two ugly sisters fighting over Prince Charming.

It was nearly 1am by the time Alice slipped into bed and the party showed no signs of ending anytime soon. She turned off the lights from the switch in the headboard, wondering briefly if Ben would know which room they were staying in, before falling into a deep sleep. She was woken around 4am by the sound of the door rattling and the keycard being scraped against the lock. She flicked on the light and let out a long sigh before hauling her tired body out of bed and opening the door. Ben half fell through the open doorway and stumbled toward the bed. Alice could smell the alcohol fumes coming from him from two metres away. "Ah, there you are," he slurred, reaching for her hand. "I missed you down there".

"Happy New Year" Alice said with a smile, leaning in to give him a peck on the cheek. Ben turned his head at the last minute to kiss her deeply on the mouth. "I'm sorry about Tish, do you forgive me?" He said, holding tightly onto both of her arms. Alice frowned, her eyebrows drawing together. "What are you talking about?" Ben was slurring, his words almost unintelligible, running into one another. She thought she made out the words 'Kissed' and 'Didn't mean it' and assumed it was Trisha who had been the lucky one who had managed to worm her way to his side at midnight.

When she managed to pull away, Alice bent down to help him with his shoelaces. He was already starting to nod off, so she spun his legs around and up onto the bed before he passed out and became a dead weight. Ben was snoring on the bed within minutes. Alice fetched a glass of water from the bathroom and put in on the side table next to him, along with a couple of paracetamols from her bag, before sliding back into bed next to him.

It was late when they both woke up the next morning. Alice heard Ben get out of bed and stumble to the toilet to throw up, she stayed where she was with her eyes closed, trying to stay asleep as long as possible. Ben returned to the bed and sat with his back propped up on the headboard and drank down the glass of water in one mouthful. "We need coffee" he said, making no attempt to get out of bed. Alice scooched up in the bed until she was sitting up next to him. She looked at her watch. "Breakfast is still open for half an hour" She said. "Are you up to eating or shall I order room service?" Ben thought about it for a few moments, before deciding. "Let's order in," he said with a groan. "The room is spinning; I could use a bit more rest." Alice nodded in agreement and picked up the phone to order coffee and orange juice. "So, you had fun last night" Alice stated with a small laugh. Ben groaned dramatically. "I think so," he said, "It's a little bit hazy." Alice smiled and put her arm around him. "So, you and Trisha......" Alice teased. Ben shot her a look, his face blanching. "What about her?" he said defensively. Alice turned to face him, surprised at the tone. "She kissed you...at midnight," she explained. "You told me when you came to bed. You were worried you had upset me." Ben's shoulders relaxed. "Oh yeah, that's what I meant," he said, with a sigh of relief. "Sorry about that. I should have stopped her, but I didn't want to upset her. It was only a kiss...." Alice looked down at her hands, thinking it through. "That's what I thought last night..." she said.

There was a knock on the door. Alice got up to let the bus boy in with their breakfast and busied herself pouring drinks for them both. She was replaying Bens words from last night over and over in her head. She had assumed he was apologising for kissing Trisha at Midnight, but now she was wondering if it was more than that. Ben had been pretty distant since she told him she was pregnant, but she had put that down to him needing some time to get used to the idea. She had ignored the fact he had been coming home from work late and working more weekends than usual. She had assumed he was busy trying to build his career and make some extra cash for the baby, but what if that had just all been excuses? She didn't know how to feel about any of this. They had argued about this a few times recently. She had complained about the amount of time he spent in the office and he had countered by saying she had become unavailable and less affectionate. She had felt guilty about that, worrying that she was becoming self-absorbed and had somehow pushed him away. Had that just been his excuse? His justification for cheating on her?

Alice carried the two cups of coffee over to the bed and handed one to Ben. She took a deep breath before asking him "Are you having an affair?" She couldn't bring herself to look at Ben, scared of what she might see in his eyes. The silence stretched out for a long minute.

"To be fair," he began "I only did it because I was unhappy." Alice couldn't believe what she was hearing. "Oh well that's ok then," she said, unable to resist the sarcasm. "As long as you had a reason, that's fine." She stood up and started to pace the room. "How long?" She asked, folding her arms across her chest, almost physically trying to hold herself together. "Was it just her or have there been others?" She continued pacing. "Actually, don't tell me. I don't want to know." She shook her head in despair while Ben just sat there looking at her, opening and closing his mouth without saying anything. She was so angry she could cry, but she was not going to give him the satisfaction.

The silence was broken by Ben's phone pinging to signal the arrival of a text. Before he could reach for it Alice snatched it up from the bedside table and looked at the incoming message. It was from Trisha, wondering if they were going to join everyone for a drink that lunchtime before heading home. Alice snorted and threw the phone on the bed in Ben's general direction. After reading the message Alice couldn't believe it when he suggested to her that they should go. "What makes you think I want to go anywhere with you right now?" Alice said to him.

"Oh come on Alice, for fucks sake. I've said I'm sorry about Trish. There's no need to ruin a perfectly pleasant invitation because of it." Daniel stood and held Alice's shoulders in an attempt to get her to stop pacing. Alice shrugged him off and moved away. "Firstly" She screamed "You have not said sorry. And secondly, I don't want to be anywhere near her, or any of your other groupies for that matter."

"I said sorry last night" said Ben through clenched teeth. Muscles bunched in his jaw and he was staring at her intensely. "And it's no bloody surprise I have to go elsewhere to get what I need when you are such a miserable cow."

Alice backed away from him a couple of footsteps, dismayed at the swing in his mood. "Anyway," He continued, bellowing at her now from the opposite side of the room, "You are not so innocent either, with your tits hanging out last night. It's obvious you were out on the pull. Fucking slut." He spat the last word at her as he stomped furiously into the bathroom. Alice stood completely still, unable to take in everything that had just happened, not sure how to react. She heard the shower turn on and the sound of clothes and belt hitting the floor. Ben opened the door again, his face still thunderous. "I am going to drinks with my friends. You can come too if you want. I don't give a shit either way." The door slammed before Alice had gathered her wits enough to formulate a response. She couldn't think of anything she wanted to do less than go to drinks with the woman or women her husband was screwing, but on the other hand she wanted to be there to make sure he was not badmouthing her and was not tempted into an action replay. She would not give those Harpies the satisfaction of thinking they had the upper hand over her.

By the time that two of them were dressed up and on their way down to drinks Alice had had a chance to calm down and the conversation between them was almost normal. Alice had time to reflect and wondered if Ben might be right after all. Maybe all this was her fault. She didn't believe he would cheat on her deliberately. If he did go with someone else it must have been because he wasn't feeling loved or cared for enough, and in Alice's mind that was all on her. She felt guilty that she had failed in her role as a girlfriend to make him happy. If he needed to see other women to get what he needed she was obviously not good enough. She vowed to try harder and to make him see how much she loved him. She was determined to be the whole woman he needed. If she could do more and be more, he wouldn't need to cheat on her with other women. Alice reached across and took Ben's hand as they walked together into the hotel bar. She would show those sluts from his office that whatever they did she could rise above it. She wore Ben's ring on her finger, and he would always come back to her.

*

Alice groaned and rolled herself out of the bed to fetch her baby from the nursery before she woke everyone else in the house up with her screaming. "It's ok bubba, Mummy's coming," she said as quietly as she could as she slipped into the room and lifted the crying infant from her basket. She sat down in the rocking chair and lifted her top so Lottie could feed. This would be so much easier if she could have the baby in the bedroom with her and Ben, but he had insisted that Lottie should sleep in the nursery. He was busy at work and didn't want to be kept awake. Alice could hear footsteps on the landing, too delicate to be Ben's. Maya popped her head around the door. "I'm going to the kitchen. Fancy a cup of tea?" she asked. "No thanks, I'm fine." Alice replied looking at her watch. 4am. "I'm so sorry to wake you this early."

"I was up anyway. The baby has had hiccups the last hour. Its driving me nuts." Maya whispered. "Are you sure you don't want anything?" Alice thought about it for a second. ", yes. A glass of milk would be lovely thanks." Maya nodded and left the room to make the drinks. She had been staying with them for a couple of weeks since Lottie was born. She was a great help around the house. She claimed she was practicing for her own baby to arrive in about two months' time. Alice thought it was probably because Maya was feeling lonely and a bit down. All her friends seemed to have abandoned her since she got pregnant, and it was taking a toll on her mental health. She loved to be the centre of attention, so being alone was close to torture for her. Ben had surprised Alice by suggesting they let Maya stay in their spare room for a while. He was not usually that friendly or easy to live with, but this arrangement seemed to be working well, and Alice had to admit she didn't know how she would have coped without her friend's support.

Alice and Ben had not spoken again about what had happened at the new year party. They had made a kind of silent pact to put it behind them and move on. Alice new it was not particularly healthy, but she was happy with the arrangement.

When Alice finally slipped back into the bed, Ben was awake and scrolling through his phone. "I hope I didn't wake you," Alice said, rolling on to her side to face him. "It wasn't you; it was the baby again. I'm sure it's trying to ruin my life," he said with a grunt of annoyance. He put the phone down on the bedside table and flicked off the light. "I need some sleep. I have a big presentation in a few hours." Alice laid in the dark for a few minutes before replying. "You keep saying 'it'," she said quietly, almost whispering. "You say 'it', and 'that baby'. You never call her by name." She turned on her lamp and sat up. "What's going on Ben?"

"I just told you I need to sleep. Turn the light off." Ben covered his eyes with his arm. Alice turned the light off but couldn't let the subject drop. "We need to talk about this Ben…"

"Fine" grunted Ben angrily. He sat up and flicked the light back on. "You really want to know what's wrong? I want a paternity test. I want proof that the baby is mine." He crossed his arms and glared at her. Alice was shocked. She realised that was staring at him with her mouth open. "Of course she is yours," she said kindly, stroking Ben's arm. "There was no-one else. You know that." Ben shook her hand off. "No, I don't know that. I only have your word for it. I have no idea if that baby is mine or not. This happens all the time. There are loads of men all over the country bringing up someone else's kid."

"Well, I'm sorry you feel that way," said Alice, laying back down and turning her back on him. Ben turned the light off and the two of them laid back to back in the dark, caught up in their own thoughts.

CHAPTER 21
ALICE 2019

Alice laid in bed in the darkened room, listening to the sounds of breakfast being prepared by Maggie. Alice knew she should get up, but it just seemed like too much effort. She had barely eaten anything for the past week and had not showered or washed her hair. Maggie had been amazing; she should get up for her sake. It was not fair to leave her to do everything for her children. She could hear Lottie at the breakfast table chattering away between mouthfuls of cereal. Alfie was in the highchair that Maggie had gone out and bought specially for him. He was babbling happily to himself. She imagined that Maggie was bustling around the kitchen in her usual, efficient way, making pancakes and coffee and entertaining the children with songs and stories. She seemed to enjoy having the children around her and had not complained once in the fortnight they had been there about being woken up by them in the night. Alfie had not yet started sleeping through the night, and Lottie had started having terrible nightmares, waking up screaming at all hours. They were all still sleeping in Maggie's bedroom. She had tidied up the spare room and moved into it to give them the bigger space.

There was a ring on the doorbell and Alice heard Maya's voice as Maggie let her in. She was obviously here to pick up Lottie. She had been taking it in turns with Maggie to take the little girl to playgroup. They had spotted Ben hanging around outside the flats several times and didn't want to leave Alice alone in case he tried to get up to see her. She was not strong enough for that yet.

She had no idea how she would react if she were to come face to face with him now. Her stomach did a sickening somersault every time she thought about it.

There was a couple of minutes of noisy activity while Lottie found her shoes and was helped into her coat before the voices moved toward the door. Everything went quiet but Alice hadn't heard the front door shut yet, so she knew Maya was still there. She assumed the two women were whispering about her, no doubt trying to decide what to do about her inability to get up. Eventually the door closed, and Maggie went back to feeding Alfie and tidying up the breakfast things.

Alice rolled over in the dingy room, but this time she was unable to go back to sleep. "Enough" she told herself out loud. "Get up now." She swung herself round to a sitting position and looked around the room. There were dirty clothes spread around every surface, hanging off the corner of the mirror and piled up next to the laundry basket. The remnants of last night's dinner were still on a tray in the corner and there was an assortment of various mugs and plates and empty baby bottles scattered randomly. She took a deep breath and stood to open the curtains. It was a bright, frosty day, and the birds were singing in the tree just outside the window. Alice gathered up as many of the clothes as she could and dumped them in the hamper and piled up all the dirty crockery to be taken out to the kitchen. She then stripped the linens off the bed and bundled them up into a manageable pile ready to be washed. With the bedroom looking a bit more reasonable, Alice stepped into the en-suite. The bathroom had escaped relatively unscathed, so Alice ran the hot water in the shower and grabbed a clean towel out of the cabinet.

Twenty minutes later with freshly brushed teeth and a set of clean clothes on, Alice felt better than she had done in a long time. She picked up the laundry hamper and headed out to the kitchen. If Maggie was surprised to see her up and about, she didn't make a big deal of it, which Alice was grateful for. She simply asked her if she would like a coffee and pointed to the cupboard where the washing powder was kept. Alice accepted the coffee and walked over to scoop Alfie out of his chair. He babbled and smiled at her and put his chubby little arms around her neck for a hug. "Mummy's here darling boy," she whispered to him. "Mummy's here now." Maggie pulled out a chair and joined Alice at the table, sliding a plate of pancakes and maple syrup across to her. As the smell of the warm butter and sugary syrup hit her nostrils Alice was suddenly aware that she was starving. Her stomach let out an audible growl. She ate two servings of the pancakes, while Maggie sat in a companionable silence opposite her. When Alice had finally finished eating and had poured herself a second cup of coffee, Maggie cleared the plates away and suggested they all move to the lounge.

"Are you feeling better?" She asked. Alice was not sure how to answer. She felt better for eating, and she didn't feel like she wanted to sleep the whole day away any more, but there was a horrible empty hole in the pit of her stomach that she didn't know how to deal with. "I think so" she replied. "At least, I feel physically better. I'm not sure how I feel about the rest of my life at the moment". Maggie nodded silently, allowing her to speak. "Truth is" continued Alice "I have never thought further than this. Than leaving him." She laced her hands together on the table. "I don't know what I'm supposed to do now. Being a single mum was never part of the plan. I don't have a job, or a house, or any way to pay for a house. I did think about moving back in with my parents, but things are not great between us. They always hated Ben, from the very beginning, so I can't go there like this. It's all too much to think about right now"

Maggie slipped down off the chair onto the floor beside Alfie and handed him a toy truck to play with. He picked it up in both hands and stuffed it into his mouth. "You don't need to leave. Stay here if you want." Maggie said, retrieving the truck that Alfie had just launched across the room. "I like having you here," she smiled. "And as for a job, I am opening the tearoom in two weeks. I can't do that all by myself. I was kind of hoping you would like to help out. What do you think?" Alice could feel tears welling at the corner of her eyes and was struggling to speak over the lump that had formed in the back of her throat. "I think you are wonderful, and I am so lucky to have you as a friend." She reached over to hug Maggie.

Maggie laughed. "You might not say that once you find out what a slave driver I am to work for." She stood up, checking her watch. "Talking of which, I have an appointment with the site manager at 10.30 to go over the final details. Do you want to come with me? I need your artistic input for the finishing touches."

"Try stopping me," Alice said with a grin.

CHAPTER 22
MAGGIE 2019

Maggie tightened the strings on her old fashioned pinny and took a last look around the tearoom to check everything was in place before opening the door to let everyone in for the first time. The workmen had done a fantastic job of transforming the industrial space into a room that was contemporary but with a bit of old-fashioned cosiness about it. The newly installed kitchen gleamed behind the full-length serving counter that housed several chiller cabinets displaying exotic assortments of cakes and scones. On the bench behind the counter was a state-of-the-art coffee machine that had cost an arm and a leg, but which Maggie was sure would be worth its weight in gold in the long run. Shelves above the counter were home to dozens of different kinds of tea leaves, from the everyday to the exotic, all of which were available to buy to take home as well as to consume on the premises. The thing that Maggie was most proud of was the full-size mural that filled one entire wall. She had commissioned Alice to produce a piece of art to complete the décor and tie all the elements of the building together, and Alice had surpassed herself. The mural, which depicted several elements of life in Smallhaven, from the glittering coastline, to the rolling hillsides inland, was a masterpiece of colour and texture, which evoked happy memories of childhood and family for Maggie. Alice gave her a thumbs up from her place behind the counter, and the three girls they had hired to be waitresses beamed at her and nodded their readiness. "Before I let everyone in. I want you to know how thankful I am for all the work you have done preparing for today. This is it now girls. Let's make this the place to be." Alice clapped, and the waitresses followed suit as the door opened with a little tinkle from the bell and the customers streamed in.

Everyone was seated quickly, and the waitresses wasted no time in circulating around the room taking orders and hurrying back and forth with cream teas, cakes, sandwiches and hot and cold drinks of all descriptions. Alice handled the orders efficiently and professionally and was in her element organising the staff and dealing with the customers. Maggie busied herself with chatting to all the guests and making sure they were happy, and giving interviews to the local press, who had all turned up to be a part of the event at her invitation. There was a happy buzz in the air and the atmosphere was warm and friendly. Everything she had dreamed it would be. The morning passed quickly. Just before lunchtime there was a lull and Maggie took the opportunity to send the girls on their breaks while she covered the tables for them. There was a tinkle at the door and Maya walked in with Lottie and Alfie. "Hiya, how lovely to see you. Hi Lottie" Maggie said, giving her a high five. She ruffled Alfie's hair. "Hello little man." She looked around Maya, her face a question. "Where's Freddie?"

"Oh, he's coming. He's with my mum, she got chatting with one of her friends outside. How's it going?" she asked, oblivious to the fact that Maggie had stopped listening to her and was intently staring at the door, waiting for Pamela Young to appear.

Maggie recognised her as soon as she stepped through the door. She had Maya's height and colouring, but there was a look around the eyes that was so familiar to Maggie she thought that everyone in the room must be aware of it.

"There you are Mum. Come in and meet Maggie. She's the one I have been telling you about. Alice's landlady" Maya said, putting her arm around her mother and steering her toward Maggie, who stood, frozen to the spot. "Alright, no need to be so bloody pushy Maya. I'm coming" Said Pamela, shrugging Mayas arm off her shoulder in annoyance. She looked at Maggie's face properly for the first time and her jaw dropped open. She was silent for a beat before regaining her equilibrium and extending her hand to Maggie. "Pleased to meet you," she said tersely, shaking Maggie's hand firmly once then dropping her hand abruptly. Maggie noticed Maya watching them with a bemused expression on her face. She pulled herself together and covered the awkward situation by pretending to see a guest who required her attention on the other side of the room. "Lovely to meet you too." Maggie said pleasantly. "I look forward to seeing you again. You are welcome here any time". Pamela's expression remained stone hard as Maggie walked away. She could faintly hear Maya behind her asking her mother why she was acting so weird. She was being beckoned by both Alice and one of her waitresses, but she was not ready to face either of them. She ducked into a cupboard and stood with her back to the door taking deep breaths, trying to steady herself.

The afternoon went well, with everyone in the tea shop singing the praises of the chef and the front of house staff. Maggie closed the door after the last afternoon tea guest at 6pm and retrieved a bottle of champagne from behind the counter to pour for the staff. "Well done everyone" she said, raising her glass in a toast. "Today went better than I ever dreamed of. You were all amazing, so thank you all and here's to us" She clinked her glass against the others as they repeated the toast. "Ok, go home, get changed and I will see you all back here in two hours for the party" she continued.

As the afternoon faded into the evening the lights went on outside reflecting in the inky black water of the river. Maggie flicked on the illuminated shop sign and plugged in the various fairy lights she had strung around the tearoom. She had arranged for a champagne cocktail bar and canapes for guests this evening and had bought a new dress in preparation. Guests had been invited from local businesses and organisations and she had asked Maya to sing for everyone. The party was due to start in an hour. Maggie sat alone in the old lifeboat station staring out to sea, watching the waves lapping gently against the harbour wall. The bell above the door tinkled as someone entered behind her. Assuming it was Alice she called out to her. "Come through, have some champagne".

Maggie turned as the footsteps stopped behind her. "It's not Alice" Said Pamela, rather unnecessarily. She took the proffered glass from Maggie's hand, but didn't take a sip. "What are you doing here Maggie?" She asked with a stony expression. "Have you come to hurt me? Is that it?" She put the glass down on the table beside her and crossed her arms tightly across her chest. "Of course not" said Maggie, genuinely hurt by the thought. "I just want to get to know you..........and my sister and nephew." She held out her free hand to touch Pamela's shoulder, but the older woman took a step back, her crossed arms a physical barrier in front of her.

"I told you five years ago; I want nothing to do with you. I don't want a relationship with you, I don't want you hanging around with my daughter and I certainly don't want you anywhere near my grandson. You need to back the hell off." Maggie's eyes stung with unwept tears. She was deeply hurt by the look of utter contempt on Pamela's face. "I just want to be part of a family. Maya has a right to know about me. I'm her sister" Maggie said.

"Don't you think that poor girl has been through enough? She doesn't need any more upset in her life." Pamela was not finished. "After Maya sings this evening that's it. You walk away from her and Freddie. No more pub nights or playgroup dates, nothing. If I find out you have so much as texted her, I will have you run out of this village. People listen to me here, so don't test me. I'm not the only one here with a secret to keep" With a dramatic swish of her long, sequinned dress, Pamela left the room leaving a stunned Maggie standing in her wake. Once she was sure she was alone Maggie allowed the tears to fall. She was angry at herself more than anything. She never should have got her hopes up. She knew Pamela didn't want to acknowledge her as a daughter, but maybe naively she thought that if they were to meet and get to know each other Pamela may be tempted to change her mind. She wiped her eyes on a napkin and stood up tall. She had a right to live there if she wanted to and could make friends with whoever she liked. She had dealt with nastier people than Pamela Young in her life.

Once the guests started arriving, Maggie had no time to worry about what had gone on between her and Pamela. The room was buzzing, and she found herself being pulled from person to person giving press statements, having photographs taken, overseeing the caterers, and chatting to guests and dignitaries. Alice's had recommended a friend of a friend, Oliver Moore, to compare the evening and he had surpassed her expectations. He was quick-witted and funny, and the audience found him warm and engaging. She had organised a silent auction to raise money for Freddie's fund, and with his expert auctioneer skills he had managed to raise over £10,000 for the cause. Shortly after that he invited Maya up to the stage to perform for them and Maggie was surprised to see him take a seat behind the baby grand piano, she had had installed for occasions such as this.

Maya sang like and angel, her voice soaring in perfect harmony with the delicate chords of Oliver's accompaniment. The pair of them received a standing ovation and Maggie made a note to book them again. They had been perfectly in sync with each other, each reading the others mind and moving through the pieces with an ease and grace that usually took many hundreds of hours practice to achieve. After giving two encores Maya finally left the stage to find Maggie. She caught up with Maggie in the stairwell and hopped toward her to give her a suffocating bear hug. "What's that for?" laughed Maggie. "You were amazing by the way. That was breath-taking"

"I have not had that much fun in years" said a breathless Maya.

"That felt fucking amazing". She hooked her arm into Maggie's and marched her in the direction of the bar. "Come on, let's get hammered". Maggie laughed, caught up in the moment. She skipped to the bar and ordered cocktails for herself and Maya, who also insisted on shots to get them started, before disappearing to use the toilet. "Don't drink without me Taylor," She shouted, "Wait for me". Grinning, Maggie swept her eyes around the room to make sure everyone was having fun. They all seemed happy to dance and drink, and the party was in full swing. She caught the eye of Pamela, when she realised that the older woman had been openly glaring at her for the past few moments. Maggie stood up tall and approached her. "I know you don't want anything to do with me Pamela, and that's fine. That's your choice. I know nothing about my birth, or my father, and that's fine if you want to keep it all a secret, but I do know about my Sister and my Nephew and I have a right to be part of their lives. I promised I wouldn't reveal who I am to them, and I mean it, but I am going to be friends with Maya and I absolutely will not walk away from her. I have no other family. You three are it and I deserve a family." Maggie caught sight of Maya coming toward them from the bathroom and removed the scowl from her face. "We can talk about this another time," she said through her fake smile. "Maya, your mother and I were just talking about your performance. She's very proud of you."

"Thanks Mum," said Maya giving her a bear hug. "I can't wait to do it again now. I've missed this. In fact, we are wasting time, let's dance" and with that she dragged her mother over to the area in front of the window that had been made into a temporary dance floor. Maggie watched the two of them for a couple of minutes. They were totally at ease with each other, and Pamela's pride and love for her daughter was written all over her face. Maggie struggled to contain the stab of jealousy she felt.

Maggie decided she needed to refill her glass. Alice was sitting beside the bar chatting to the pianist from earlier, when he saw her, he stood an offered his hand to shake. "Oliver Moore" he said. "Pleased to meet you at last. Alice here has been singing your praises" Maggie smiled and nodded her thanks to Alice. "Talking of singing praises, thank you so much for the music earlier. It was just gorgeous. You are very talented." Oliver blushed, and looked to the floor, clearly embarrassed by the compliment. "Thank you" he said, "but it's easy to sound good when there is such a fantastic vocalist..."

"She is good isn't she" Maggie stated, with a touch of pride. Maya may not know that they were related, but Maggie had had 5 years to adjust to having a secret sister and she found it easy to be proud of Maya's accomplishments, even though the other wasn't even aware she was alive. "Yes. I used to teach her you know before she went on Britain's got Talent." Oliver said. "I didn't know she was on there" answered Maggie in surprise. She was sure she would know something like that. She had been following Maya on social media for years. "Actually" piped up Alice, "She did really well. Got the golden buzzer through to the next round, but then she had to pull out, so they didn't show it on television. She has a copy of the audition though. I'm sure she would show you."

"I will ask her" Maggie said. She had not realised how talented Maya was. What a shame that she had had to give up on her dreams. No wonder she came across as a bitch sometimes. She could see now that she had a lot to be bitchy about.

By eleven o'clock most of the guests had left. The caterers began packing up and cleaning around the few stragglers that remained. Alice and Oliver were still sat beside the bar, where they had been for the majority of the evening, deep in conversation. The pair of them were drunk, so Maggie nipped behind the counter and into the kitchen to make double espressos for them both. The sound of raised voices and a piercing scream sent her running back where she came from. Alice was on the floor, holding on to Oliver who appeared to be unconscious and was bleeding from a cut on his cheekbone. Two of the bar staff were holding on to Ben who had appeared from somewhere, trying to remove him bodily from the building. He appeared to be drunk, and his right hand was bleeding from where he had hit Oliver. He was red in the face and shouting unintelligibly. Maggie could make out odd swear words and insults that were directed at Alice. Maggie crouched down to check on Oliver. He had regained consciousness and the cut didn't seem that deep, but he probably needed to go to hospital. She shouted instructions to a waitress who was watching open mouthed from behind the counter. "Call the police, and an ambulance. And pass me that first aid box." She took a handful of napkins from the table to staunch the flow of blood from Oliver's face. "Hold this here" she directed Alice, who had gone completely white and was beginning to shake uncontrollably. "You are ok, do you hear me?" she shouted at her, to get her attention. "Look after Oliver, you are fine" She said as she stood and marched across the room to where Ben was still fighting to break free from the two waiters who were holding him. With arms outstretched she pushed his chest, forcing him backwards toward the open door. She was so angry she could hear her heart beating in her ears. The surge of adrenaline gave her strength "Get away from her, you bully" She screamed at him. He stumbled over his own feet, shocked into silence. He stopped fighting for a second and the two men took advantage of that to sweep him up off his feet to dump him on the pavement outside. Maggie bolted the door behind them when they came back in and returned to Oliver and Alice. Suki the waitress had taken over looking after Oliver while Melanie was on the phone directing the police where to come. Alice had sat back on her knees and was sobbing on the floor. "It's ok. You're safe" said Maggie "You're safe, Oliver is going to be fine. You're safe" She helped Alice up onto a chair, while reassuring her, and asked Melanie to fetch the espressos she had been making.

The police and paramedic arrived in a couple of minutes and bundled Ben into the back of a car. Oliver didn't need stitches, so once he was cleaned up and had a dressing applied Maggie called a taxi for him. As she helped him into it later, she thanked him again for his part in the evening. "I'm so sorry it had to end like this" She said, stroking his arm and nodding toward his battered face. "It was lovely to meet you." Oliver leaned in to give her a hug before getting into the taxi. "It was lovely meeting you too. Take care of Alice." Maggie assured him that she would and waved him off. She returned to the shop to give her statement to the police and oversee the caterers who had almost finished cleaning up and needed paying before they left.

Alice was in no state to speak to the police, or anyone, that evening. The upset and the alcohol had taken their toll. Maggie gave a swift overview of what had happened and arranged for her and Alice to go to the police station in the next few days to file a proper statement. Maggie shut and locked the shop and walked arm in arm with Alice along the river toward home, neither of them said a word as they both replayed the evening's events over in their minds.

CHAPTER 23
ALICE 2019

Alice stopped on the stairs and closed her eyes, her hands clenching and unclenching at her sides. She couldn't catch her breath and she wondered if she might fall. "Are you ok?" asked Maggie from a spot just behind her. Alice answered yes automatically, unable to form any other words. She was sweating, even though the day was cool. She became aware of Maggie's hand on her back guiding her up the stairs and she listened to her voice telling her to breathe and stay calm. They crossed the threshold into the police station together and Maggie steered her toward the seating area before leaving her, presumably to check in. Alice dropped her head down to her knees and concentrated on taking slow deep breathes until the pounding of her heart in her ears quieted enough for her to hear other sounds. Calmer now, she consciously listened to the sounds of the station, bringing her breathing under control. By the time Maggie returned with a plastic cup full of cold-water Alice was feeling better. "Thanks for the water" she said, draining the cup and putting it on the table beside her. Maggie took her hand "Are you sure you are ready for this?" she asked, a concerned look on her face. Alice knew she looked a mess. She had not slept at all the night before, and the tiredness combined with the hangover that was starting to form behind her eyes was not helping. She knew that she had to do this now though. If she waited even one more day, she would never be able to pluck up the courage again. "I'm fine Maggie, honestly." She reassured her friend, sounding more convinced than she felt. "Thanks for being here with me." Maggie nodded solemnly in response and gave her hand a squeeze as a female police officer called them in to an interview room.

The room was almost completely bare. The only thing on the wall was a poster about where to meet in case of a fire. There was a small table in the middle of the room with two plastic chairs on either side. A small, square window provided a view out to the carpark beyond. The woman introduced herself as PC Wanda Bailey. She was younger than Alice and had an efficient manner about her. She had a notepad and pen in front of her and as she asked Alice questions, she made a note of the answers in longhand. Although this made the process rather slow Alice was glad as it gave her time to think over her answers and keep herself calm as they talked. Maggie had taken a seat just behind Alice, sitting against the back wall. She appreciated that. She wanted to know Maggie was there to support her, but she couldn't bear to see her friends face when she spoke about all that she had been through. She didn't want to see disgust or anger in Maggie's eyes, she didn't want to feel judged or pitied. All she wanted was to lay out the facts of the story as clearly and concisely as she could and get it all off her chest. She had a tight hold on herself at the moment, any hint of sympathy or pity and she may just unravel.

"So, Alice, do you think you could start by telling me when the abuse began?" PC Bailey asked, pen poised. Alice placed both hands flat on the table in front of her and studied the backs of her fingers intently. "Everything was great for the first few months. We moved in together really quickly. We were in love. Ben was just setting up his own estate agency and I had enrolled on a Fine Art degree at the Uni. He was always a bit jealous of me speaking to other men, and at first I didn't mind. I found it kinda flattering actually." Alice flicked her eyes up to check that Wanda was keeping up with her. She nodded for Alice to continue. "But then he started getting jealous of my female friends. It started getting ridiculous. He didn't like me dressing too sexy and he always wanted to know where I was and who I was speaking to. It got too difficult to go out. I couldn't be bothered arguing. So I stayed in more and more. He didn't of course. He was out all the time drinking and flirting, but he thought that was ok. And I didn't stop him so…," Alice trailed off, staring out at the blank square of tarmac. "Then I got pregnant. I didn't mean to. It was an accident, one of those things. I wanted to keep it, and I thought he did too. But then he started asking all the time if the baby was his. Accusing me of seeing other people, of sleeping with other men." Alice looked up at Wanda, who returned her gaze. "It was his. Both the kids are his. I have never even been with another man ever. But he just wouldn't accept that." She dropped her eyes back to her fingers which were now clenched together on her lap. "That's when I found out he had had an affair." Alice heard a small, sharp intake of breath from Maggie behind her, but she chose to ignore it. "He started staying out real late and giving me all these excuses about having to work late and taking clients out to dinner. And I was such an idiot I believed him. But then I found some other woman's knickers in his trouser pocket when I did the laundry. I confronted him about it and he said it was my fault. Said I had been ignoring him. Giving all my attention to my pregnancy. He said I was boring." She shook her head at the memory. "I had a hard pregnancy with Lottie. I threw up all the time and was just so tired. I gave up my course. I just didn't have the energy for it. Ben carried on coming home late, smelling of booze and perfume, and honestly, I didn't even care. I was just glad someone else was keeping him occupied. But then Lottie came." Alice smiled, and pulled up a picture of the new-born Charlotte on her phone to hold out for Wanda to see. "She was a beautiful baby. But she was not an easy one. She cried all the time and I just couldn't seem to stop her. Looking back, I realise now that I had postnatal depression, but you can never see it at the time. Ben started getting stroppy. He blamed me for Lottie keeping him awake so I started sleeping in the nursery with her so I could get to her in the night before she woke him up. Then he started accusing me of having an affair again. He thought I must be seeing someone else because I didn't sleep in the bed with him and he accused me of sleeping with everyone. If the postman chatted to me on the doorstep Ben would be furious with me after. Screaming in my face, calling me a whore." She looked back at Wanda to make sure she was still listening. She nodded for Alice to continue. "That's when he started raping me. He wanted sex all the time. If I was too tired or just didn't want to, he screamed at me and accused me of getting it elsewhere, so most of the time I just let him get on with it. A couple of times when I said no, he got rough and did it anyway." Tears formed in her eyes, but she rubbed them away with the back of her hand. "If I cried or got upset, he laughed at me. He called me a whore. Said that was all I was good for. So, I just let him do it. It was easier than arguing." Alice heard Maggie sniffle behind her. "Anyway, one particularly bad night he came home late from the pub. Drunk as usual. Lottie had colic and was not sleeping. I was tired and stressed out and I said no. I walked away from him to see to the baby and he got mad. He followed me into the nursery and grabbed Lottie out of my arms. He was screaming at me, saying I loved Lottie more than him and he wished she had never been born. He was shaking her. I thought he was going to kill her, and she was just screaming and screaming." Alice put her hands over her ears, eyes closed. "I tried to grab her from him. I was hitting his arms trying to make him let go. He threw the baby into the cot and I managed to get her and run into the bathroom. It was the only door with a lock. I shut us in there and sat against the door. He banged and shouted so much that the neighbours got worried and knocked on the door. He got rid of them somehow and must have fallen asleep downstairs, because he didn't come back up. I slept there all night with Lottie, in the bath, with a towel as a pillow. The next day he came home from work nice as pie. He apologised. Gave me flowers. Told me he loved me, and spent the evening playing with Lottie and giving her cuddles. He promised me things would be better between us. And I believed him, like a bloody idiot. Even when he took the lock off the bathroom door." Alice reached for a tissue from the box on the table and wiped her eyes. "Ok," said Wanda. "How about we take a break? Can I get you some coffee? Or water?" Alice nodded and agreed to some coffee. Maggie asked for water and pulled her chair up next to Alice as Wanda left the room. "You are doing great," she told Alice, putting her arm around her shoulder. Alice looked at her. She had been crying. Her eyes were red and watery. Alice handed her a tissue. "It's ok you know. I really am fine," she reassured her friend. "It's good to finally say it all out loud." Maggie just nodded and hugged her tighter.

Alice felt more relaxed during the second half of the interview. She explained to the police officer how Ben had systematically isolated her from all of her friends and family. How he had gradually knocked her confidence and self-esteem down to the extent that she started to believe that she deserved the way he was treating her. She felt that no one else would ever love her. They fell into a sort of truce. As long as she behaved the way she knew Ben wanted her to, things seemed to be ok. He was charming and fun, the life and soul of the party whenever they went out. He was well liked and respected in the community and no one ever suspected that things were anything other than harmonious at home. Ben was more discreet about his affairs with other women, but Alice knew he was still seeing people behind her back. She was past caring. If she had to endure a pitying look from the women at his agency who knew he was screwing around, that was ok. She could cope with that. She told Wanda that she had thought about leaving him several times, but he had control of all of their finances. She had no friends, no money, no car and nowhere to go. She was his hostage. And with two kids to look after she was in no position to leave him. Everyone in town thought he was fantastic, so it's not like she could just run and throw herself on their mercy. She was well and truly trapped. But then she had met Maggie, and things had changed. She turned in her chair and took Maggie's hand. "I owe you my life….and my children's lives." Tears spilled out of Maggie's eyes and she pulled Alice in for a hug. Alice allowed herself to cry for the first time in a long time, holding Maggie tightly. "I've got you," said Maggie. "I've got you. You're safe now."

CHAPTER 24
MAYA 2019

Maya could tell something was wrong the minute she walked into the house. Her mum had been baking. That could mean only one thing. She had something on her mind, and that could never be good. "Go and hug Grandma", Maya whispered to Freddie, hoping he would diffuse the tension. Pamela could never stay angry or upset when her grandson was around. Maya hung up their jackets then wandered into the kitchen to join her mother and son. By the time she got in there Freddie was already standing on a step stool helping Pamela to mix up a huge batch of butter icing for her cupcakes. She smiled as she watched the concentration on his little face as he tried not to spill any of the mixture. "How's things Mum?" she asked, giving her a kiss on the cheek. "Is something on your mind?"

"Well actually dear there is. You must be able to read my mind" Pamela wiped her hands on her apron and took a sip from her cup of tea. "I have something to tell you, but it will have to wait until little ears are somewhere else", she indicated Freddie with a nod of her head. "Hey Freddie," said Maya, "How about we go and find Grandad and see if he wants to play football at the park?" Freddie jumped off the stool and threw his apron onto the back of the kitchen chair, before running to the lounge to find his Grandad. Pamela chuckled as she watched him leave. "I don't know what I would do without that little boy," she said while pouring Maya a cup of tea and indicating that they should sit at the kitchen table. Maya took the cup and pulled out a chair facing the window so she could watch Freddie in the garden. "Ok Mum spit it out, whatever it is". Pamela handed her a coaster, which she slipped underneath her mug, waiting for her to start talking.

Pamela pulled out a chair opposite her daughter and sat down with a sigh. "You know I don't like to interfere in your life" she began to Maya's amusement, "but, that friend of yours is bad news. You need to stay away from her." Pamela rang her hands together as she spoke. Maya watched her, confused. "Alice? You think Alice is bad news?" Maya replied.

"What? No, of course not. I love Alice" said Pamela. "I'm talking about the new one.... Maggie. There are things about her that you don't know, bad things. It's not safe for my Grandbaby to be around her. She's dangerous." Pamela held eye contact with Maya, emphasising how important this was to her. Maya raised her eyebrows, "Mother, what are you talking about. How can she be dangerous? She used to be a schoolteacher...."

"I know that" Pamela interrupted "But there's a reason why she isn't a schoolteacher anymore. And that reason is why I don't want her near Freddie anymore. And I need you to listen to me" Maya was getting impatient now. "Look Mum," She said, closing her eyes to attempt to stay calm. "How about you just say what you want to say, get it over with, and I will decide whether she is a danger to my child or not?"

"She's a paedophile." Pamela blurted out. Maya looked at her open mouthed. "What the fuck?"

"Well technically, her husband was the paedo." Pamela clarified. "But she was definitely an accomplice. I read about it in the newspaper a while back." Maya didn't know what to say. She couldn't process the words she was hearing. She didn't even know Maggie was married. But then thinking about it, what did she know about Maggie's past? The more she thought about it, the more she realised that she knew nothing about the woman who had become a big part of her and her son's life recently. "Ok. Tell me everything you know." Maya said, paying attention properly now. Pamela leant forward across the table. "Well, her and her husband had their foster kids taken away from them after he forced himself on the pre-teen daughter," she almost whispered, as if they were conspiring together. "They were never convicted of anything, but he killed himself over it, so that says all you need to know doesn't it." She sat back, watching Maya to see how the news had affected her.

Maya shook her head. "Are you sure you have the right person?" She watched Freddie in the garden kicking a ball around with her Dad. She crossed her arms, two small lines forming between her eyes as she frowned in confusion. "She's great with Freddie. She's a natural. He loves her."

"Look," said Pamela, holding her hands up "If you don't believe me, google it." Maya thought about it for a minute. If there was any chance that this was true, she should find out everything she could about it. Pamela left to join her husband playing with Freddie. She returned ten minutes later to find Maya in tears at the kitchen table.

Maya felt sick. She was staring at the news page. Maggie had changed her hair and was wearing glasses, but the person in the picture was definitely her. For weeks now she had been letting Maggie look after Freddie. She had helped her in the tearoom and treated her like a friend. And now she finds out that Maggie had a whole secret life that she knew nothing about. The more she thought about it the more she realised the extent that Maggie had wheedled her way into Maya's life, and how much time she spent with Freddie. Maggie had been the one to pursue her friendship, not the other way around. It all made sense to her now.

"Oh my god, Alice" She said, fighting a bout of nausea. "Alice and the kids." She put her hands over her mouth. "I need to speak to Alice Mum, now. Look after Freddie for me please. I have to go and warn her who she's living with." Maya gathered up her bag and keys and ran toward the door. "I'll be back later."

"Ok dear" said Pamela, managing to hide her satisfaction, "He's safe with us. Take as long as you need."

Maya's mind was racing as she drove toward Maggie's house. She felt betrayed. She was not the type to make friends easily and this just proved to her that she was right to be careful. You could never trust people. She pulled up in the carpark way too fast and slammed on the brakes as she pulled into the space nearest the door. She couldn't see Maggie's car anywhere, so she assumed she was working at the tearoom. She pressed every button on the intercom until someone buzzed her in to the building and ran up to the top floor taking the stairs two at a time. She pounded on the door until Alice opened it. "Oh, thank fuck, you're here" she said as Alice stepped aside to let her in. "Maya, what's wrong?" she said with a worried expression on her face. "Is it Freddie? Where is he? What's wrong?" She was close to panic.

"Where's Maggie?" Maya said, changing the subject. "Where are the babies? Are the kids ok?"

"Of course they're ok," said Alice, "You are freaking me out, Maya. What's going on?"

"Where's Maggie? Is she here?" Maya repeated, grabbing Alice by the shoulders.

Alice was shaking. Her face deathly pale. "No, she's at work. She'll be home at 7 if you want her?"

Maya shook her head and relaxed her shoulders, letting her arms drop to her sides. "No, I don't want her. I never want to speak to that lying bitch ever again," she said with venom. She took a breath to centre herself so she could speak calmly to Alice. "Let's have a cup of tea. I need to show you something. Something bad." She took Alice's arm, leading her into the kitchen. "Then I will help you pack your stuff up before Maggie gets home."

Alice was looking at her as if she were becoming unhinged, but

Maya couldn't help that. She had to make her understand so the kids wouldn't be left with that woman for another minute. Two hours later, Maya took the key from Alice, whose hands were shaking too much to insert it into the lock. She closed the door and posted the key back through the letterbox. She helped Alice load the rest of Alice's things into her car, before driving Alice and the two kids back to her parent's house.

CHAPTER 25
MAGGIE 2018

Maggie pulled up outside Soraya's school twenty minutes early for her meeting with the head teacher, so she parked the car and took the opportunity to call the social worker again. As per the previous two calls she had put through the phone went straight to voicemail. "Hi Vivien. Its Maggie again. Please could you call me back as soon as you can? We are having some issues with Soraya. I could use your advice". She sighed and slipped the phone back into her bag, ready to go in and face the music. This was the third time in a month she had been called into the school due to Soraya's behaviour and she was willing to admit that she felt out of her depth. She signed in at reception and was buzzed through into a brightly lit corridor that was filled with displays of children's artwork. She took a seat in the waiting area but had barely had time to sit down before the headteacher's personal assistant came around the corner to collect her. "Good morning Mrs Taylor" she said to Maggie, extending a hand for her to shake. "Please follow me." Maggie did as instructed; not bothering to reply. She had attempted to engage the efficient PA in conversation previously, only to be shut down. She assumed that the woman didn't want to get involved in conversations about children without the headteacher being present. Either way, Maggie was happy to be silent. She was struggling to control her emotions. She understood that Soraya was just pushing the boundaries, trying to find out how far she could go before Maggie and Daniel would give up on her. Maggie felt so sad for the child, wishing she could make her understand that she was safe and loved. Unfortunately, years of experience had taught Soraya that that was not always the case, so she often presented as difficult. She could be argumentative and rude, and Maggie had caught her in a lie many times recently. She understood how hard life had been for Soraya, and this was just her way of getting through it. She was still in survival mode, and she couldn't trust that things had changed for her yet. Maggie wished she could help the little girl overcome these issues. She was willing to take however long it needed to make Soraya feel safe again. On the other hand, Maggie was fuming. She and Daniel had bent over backwards for Soraya and she had done nothing to help them. She didn't want to be angry at her. She knew that it was pointless, and was not going to help, but she just couldn't stop herself feeling cross and disappointed and that made her feel like a bad mother.

"Welcome, Mrs Taylor, thank you for coming in at such short notice." the head teacher Mr Matthews said as she entered his office. She nodded to him and took a seat opposite him. Soraya was already there. She was sat with her feet up on the chair, hugging her knees. She had been crying but the look on her face now was pure anger. Maggie pulled her chair a little closer to Soraya and put her hand on her back. "Put your feet down please Soraya and sit up straight. Be respectful." She handed her foster child a tissue and turned her attention to Mr Matthews. He didn't wait for her to ask before telling her what had happened. "Soraya has been in a fight this morning with one of her classmates. We have done a full investigation and it seems that Soraya took a biscuit bar from another child's lunch box and ate it. She lied to the teacher in charge about what she had done. Later at playtime she found the child who the biscuit belonged to and punched him for telling on her." He held Maggie's gaze to make sure she was listening to him. "This is a serious matter. We don't take violence and fighting lightly in this school. In line with our anti-bullying policy Soraya is going to have to be excluded for a day." He stopped talking, his fingers steepled together, eyes peering over the top of his clasped hands. Maggie turned to Soraya. "Is this true? Is there something you would like to say?" she asked her. Soraya's frown deepened into a scowl. "Yes, it's true, and no I don't want to say anything," she said before turning to stare out of the open window. Maggie turned her chair to face her daughter. "Soraya, this is important. You can't just go around hurting people whenever you feel like it and taking their things. There are rules that you must follow. And when you don't follow them there are consequences." Soraya looked at her, defiant. Maggie almost lost her resolve. She could see through the anger. She knew that Soraya was hurting. Something was obviously upsetting her, and she could tell that this acting up was just a front, a way of avoiding her real feelings. Now was not the time to back down though. "Ok Soraya, you are going to spend tomorrow writing an apology letter to the child you hurt. You are then going to do your homework." Soraya rolled her eyes and crossed her arms. "Plus, you will not be going horse-riding for the next two weekends." That had the effect that Maggie was waiting for. Soraya stood up fists clenched at her sides. "No, not fair" she screamed. "Not fair. I hate you". Maggie turned her attention back to the head teacher. "I'm sorry about this Mr Matthews. I assume there is a return to school meeting on Monday?"

"Yes, thank you Mrs Taylor. 9am sharp." Mr Matthews nodded his thanks to her then looked at Soraya. "Soraya, I want you to understand, we love having you in our school. You are a very bright young lady, and you will do well here. But we will not tolerate bad behaviour here. When you come back on Monday it will be a fresh start. Make good choices. For now, I would like you to wait outside my office while I speak to your mum." He stood up and walked around the desk to see Soraya to the door, then turned back to Maggie. "Mrs Taylor. I'm sure I don't need to tell you how difficult this situation is. We have put lots of support in for Soraya, but she is fighting us all the way. I would like your permission to make an appointment for her with our counsellor. I think it might help. Mrs Rose has had good results with some of our other looked after children." Maggie nodded. "Yes of course, whatever you think," she replied. "I have called the social worker as well. I'm hoping she can give us some advice. And I'm so sorry about this. I will talk to her tonight. Thank you." Mr Matthews nodded and shook her hand. He opened the office door. Soraya was sitting cross legged on the chair outside the door, her head in her hands. She stood up as Maggie walked out to meet her. "Goodbye Soraya," Said Mr Matthews. "I will see you both on Monday".

Maggie took Soraya by the hand and they walked in silence to the car. Maggie had to find a way of dealing with this so that they could both win. The social workers and other foster parents on the training course had warned her that this behaviour was normal, but it didn't make it any easier to deal with. Neither one of them said anything on the journey home. Once they were in the house Soraya ran straight up to her bedroom and slammed the door. Maggie decided to leave her there to give her time to think about what had happened.

When Daniel got home two hours later with the twins, Soraya was still in her room. Maggie was cooking dinner in the kitchen. He walked over and kissed her on the cheek. "You're home early. Everything ok?" He helped the boys take off their coats and strapped them both into the chairs at the dining table and handed them drinks and pieces of apple. Maggie kissed the boys hello and sat at the table with them. "There was an incident at school today," she told Daniel. "Soraya hit a child and stole from her. She's excluded tomorrow." Daniel was always the calm one in the relationship. He took a minute to process what she had just told him. "Where is she now?" He asked. "She's upstairs thinking about what she did" Maggie replied. She explained to him what had happened during the meeting and the two of them chatted about what they should do. They agreed that it would be the best thing for Daniel to miss work the next day to look after her. As Maggie was her favourite person, they decided that Soraya may find it more of a reward than a punishment to spend the whole day with her. Daniel went up to her room to give her the news. Maggie could tell the conversation wasn't going well. She could hear Soraya shouting and throwing things from where she was. They were not in for an easy evening.

As soon as the clock struck 12 the next day Maggie sent her class out to play and made her way to the staff room as quickly as she could. She had had to leave for work before Soraya was up that morning. She was teaching all day and needed to go in early to prep. The nanny came to take the twins to day care as usual so Daniel could be at home to supervise Soraya. Maggie couldn't concentrate on her work. All morning she had been distracted and on edge. She called Daniel's mobile. She knew it was not fair to micromanage him as he was perfectly capable of looking after Soraya, and she didn't want him to think she didn't trust him, but she knew she would not be able to relax if she didn't at least check. She tried twice but got voicemail both times. She left a message asking him to call her back. She grabbed her lunch bag from the fridge and flicked on the kettle. Her friend Judy was sat in the corner and had been watching her quietly. "Coffee would be great thanks Mags," she said, by way of getting Maggie's attention. "What was all that about? Trouble at home?" Maggie knew that anyone listening in to their conversation would have thought that sounded rude, but they had known each other for ages and could read each other's moods. She listened thoughtfully and tried to reassure her that everything was going to be ok, but still Maggie could not shake this feeling that something was wrong. As soon as her staff meeting was over at the end of the day, Maggie raced home.

When she got in all three children were eating their dinner at the table in the kitchen. The twins were pleased to see her. She gave them both a kiss on the top of their heads and walked around the table to Soraya. The little girl turned her head away and carried on eating in silence. "Still mad at me huh?" said Maggie. She turned her attention to Daniel, who was putting the finishing touches to a pie he was assembling. "How's your day been?" she asked, wrapping her arms around his waist, and indicating to Soraya with her eyes. He kissed her on the nose and pushed her gently away with his forearms to avoid touching her with his floury hands. "Quiet, mostly" He laughed. "We have been taking part in a silent process most of the day. All homework and chores have been done though, so it's all good. A bit of silence was quite nice actually. We don't get much of that around here anymore." Maggie smiled in agreement, "We certainly don't." She wiped the boy's hands as they finished their meal and helped them down from the table. "How long until we eat?" she asked Daniel.

"About an hour. Are you hungry now? I could make you a snack?" He replied.

"No, that's fine. I am going to bath the kids and do stories. You relax for a bit," she said, taking the boys hands and leading them toward the stairs. "Are you coming for a bath Soraya?" she asked the little girl with a smile. Soraya clearly wanted to say no and hold on to her bad mood, but a smile crept to the corners of her mouth and she skipped to the stairs to race the boys into the bathroom.

An hour later all three children were asleep in bed, so Maggie and Daniel settled down to eat the meal he had prepared. They had just finished the starter when there was a shriek from the top of the stairs. "I've got a headache." Soraya was standing at her bedroom door screaming. Maggie and Daniel jumped out of their chairs and ran up the stairs. Maggie stopped to see to Soraya while Daniel checked to make sure the boys were ok. "What's wrong Babygirl?" said Maggie, checking Soraya's temperature with the back of her hand. She didn't seem too hot, but she was red in the face from screaming. "Ok, ok, you need to calm down now. Take a breath, use your words and tell me what's wrong" Maggie sat down on the top step and rocked Soraya on her lap, stroking her hair to calm her. "I've got headache." She sobbed. "And my tummy hurts." She looked up at Maggie's face, tears in her eyes. "I think I would feel better downstairs with you."

"Well, I think the best thing if you are feeling poorly is to rest in your own bed, nice and snuggly. How about we get you a drink of water and see if you can fall back to sleep?" Soraya reluctantly agreed and padded along the landing to her room. Maggie followed her in, tucked her into bed and kissed her goodnight again. "I will see you in the morning. Remember you need to go to sleep to make your headache go away." Soraya looked forlorn and rolled away from Maggie, her face to the wall. Maggie patted her on the shoulder and made sure her night light was on as she left the room and closed the door. Daniel was waiting outside on the landing. "Is everything ok?" he asked, following Maggie down the stairs. Maggie turned and smiled at him. "Yes, I think someone is feeling a bit left out. She will be ok. I don't think she's ill, its attention seeking. Probably because of what happened today." Daniel nodded and agreed that she was probably right.

The two of them had barely started on their main course before they were disturbed again, this time by Soraya coming into the kitchen with her empty water cup asking for another drink. This time Daniel took her back upstairs to bed. Soraya was slow to settle down and managed to get herself wound up to a such a state that she made herself sick. Daniel called Maggie upstairs and he stripped the bed while Maggie showered Soraya off and dressed her in clean pyjamas. "Listen to me now Soraya," Said Maggie, in what she hoped was a stern but kind tone of voice, "you are being silly, making yourself feel sick. You are very tired, and you need to go to sleep. You are safe here. You know that don't you?" Soraya looked at Maggie with sad eyes and reached her hand up to touch Maggie's face. "I just want you to stay with me in my room," she said. "I don't feel sick when you are in my room." Maggie sighed, it was getting late and her meal with Daniel was ruined already. She didn't want Soraya to be unhappy and she didn't want her screaming the place down and waking the twins up all night. "Ok, just this once. Wait here while I get my pyjamas on." Soraya nodded and Maggie left the room. Daniel had followed her up the stairs and had evidently been listening outside the door as he had gathered a blanket and pillows for her to make up a bed on the sofa in Soraya's room. "It's just for tonight," Maggie said to him, kissing him on the cheek and giving his hand a squeeze. "I know" he said. "whatever it takes." They smiled at each other and headed their separate ways.

Things didn't improve much the following night, and by Sunday evening Maggie felt as though she was living in a war zone. Soraya had been moody and difficult since leaving school on Thursday. She asked every half an hour if she could go horse-riding and every time she was told no she found ever more imaginative ways to cause disruption and chaos in the house. She broke all her toys, threw all her possessions from her room out of the window and prodded and poked the twins when she had an opportunity, making them cry. Maggie left several calls with their social worker requesting advice. She drew on all her teacher training but every tactic she tried, failed. She was not used to having children defy her, this was new. In her head she knew that Soraya was just acting out and testing boundaries, but she was tired from two nights of very poor sleep. Out of desperation she called Daniel to the bedroom for a discussion. "She's not listening to me at all now." Maggie started. "I can't get her to stop screaming and shouting for long enough to listen to a word I say. I can't sleep in there for one more night. It's just going to get worse. We are going to have to put our foot down." She sounded far more confident about the statement than she felt. "One of us needs to be bad cop" she said, wincing. She knew Daniel would not be happy about it, but she also knew it had to be him. He had taken a backseat over the past few days to look after the twins, so she had been trying to win Soraya round. It wouldn't make sense for her to start getting tough now. Daniel rolled his eyes. "Ok, I'll do it," he said, with a defeated look on

175

his face. "But you have to be bad cop for both the twins."

"It's a deal," she agreed. They both went downstairs and waited by the door for the inevitable footsteps. True to form Soraya came trotting out of her room, cup in hand, with the excuse of needing more water. Daniel bounded up the stairs before she had a chance to get past the top step and ushered her back into her bed. He pasted a stern look on his face, "Enough is enough, now Soraya. You are going to bed and I don't want to hear another peep out of you until the morning." Maggie was impressed. She had never heard him raise his voice. She heard the bedroom door click shut and popped her head around the door to see how Daniel was. He was leaning against Soraya's door with his head against the wood, trying to listen. After a few minutes he nodded and sneaked down the stairs back to Maggie.

The good cop/ bad cop routine seemed to work surprisingly well. Maggie and Daniel had spoken about it in bed the previous night. Maggie was worried that Soraya had responded to it because she was used to being shouted at, and she hated that they had had to resort to punishment, when they had originally planned to be the kind of parents who encouraged and rewarded good behaviour rather than punishing the bad. Daniel agreed, but he was also pragmatic enough to point out that none of them had slept properly for three nights and that was not healthy either. In the end Maggie agreed with his assessment that it had been necessary to get tough with Soraya, and she had to admit, she felt a hell of a lot better for having a good night's sleep.

Daniel was downstairs feeding the children pancakes by the time she finished showering and got dressed that morning. She was pleased to see that Soraya was chatting with Daniel and her brothers and seemed none the worse for the incident. They ate a relaxed breakfast as a family before Daniel left to take the boys to day care.

In the car on the way to their post exclusion meeting Maggie took the opportunity to talk to Soraya once more about her behaviour at school. Soraya appeared to listen and seemed genuinely sorry about hurting the other child. She clutched her hand-written apology note in one hand and her lunch bag in the other as they waited outside the head teacher's office. As soon as Mr Matthews opened the door to invite them in Soraya handed him the letter and told him how sorry she was for behaving badly. Maggie felt a sharp burst of pride and couldn't help smiling at her little girl who had managed to work out her feelings and come to a sensible decision. After the meeting, Maggie waved Soraya goodbye and almost skipped to her car with relief. She dialled Daniel hands free as she was driving and told him what had happened. They agreed to take the children out to the park together that evening then to get some pizza as a special treat. When she put the phone down Maggie sang along to the radio and was still singing as she walked into her class-room half an hour later.

CHAPTER 26
ALICE 2019

Alice's mobile was vibrating off the table. She didn't need to look at it to know that it was Maggie calling her. She had left ten voicemail messages in the past two days, each one getting more and more desperate. She pressed the decline button and shoved the phone into the bottom of her bag. She knew she would have to confront her at some point, but right now she was still too angry and upset to speak. Just when she thought she had started to regain some of her power and spirit by leaving Ben, she had taken her kids out of one dangerous situation and placed them in another that was potentially even worse. She didn't know if she would be able to forgive Maggie for that.

Alice decided to jump in the shower while the kids were still sleeping. Maybe the hot water would wash some of the fatigue from her. She needed to be on top of her game today. She was going to meet an agency, who could potentially set her up with a job. Maya had been great letting her and the kids stay there, but the situation was not ideal. There was only one bedroom, which she was using with the two children. Maya and Freddie were sleeping in the lounge on a pull-out sofa bed. Fine for a few nights, but by no means a long-term solution. She needed a job and money of her own if she were to maintain her newfound independence.

Alice absentmindedly picked up toys from the bedroom floor and placed them in the lidded toybox. She hefted the suitcase up from the floor to place on the top and selected clean clothes for the children out of it, ready for them when they woke up. She had never known the children to sleep so long, or so deeply. They were usually both up by 5am. Maybe they had picked up more of what was going on before than she realised. She was glad Lottie was still asleep as Alice couldn't face all her questions right now. Lottie missed Maggie terribly. The two of them had formed a strong bond and Lottie was desperate to see her.

Alice crept into the kitchen past Maya and Freddie who were snuggled together on the sofa. Maya stirred as she passed her. "Coffee" she croaked "I need coffee. Bad night" she said by way of explanation. Alice nodded and continued into the kitchen to put on a pot of coffee. Maya joined her a few minutes later, pulling herself up onto a stool at the counter and stirring three large spoonsful of sugar into her coffee. "Is Freddie ok?" Alice asked.

"Yeah I think so. Just a tummy ache." She drank down half her coffee in one gulp. "I just can't help worrying that it's something worse you know?"

Alice blushed, suddenly ashamed of herself. "I'm so sorry Maya. Here I am complaining about my life and I forget that you have been through so much worse with Freddie. I've been so selfish..."

"Hey. You don't need to do that. It's not a competition who got handed the biggest shit sandwich." Maya stirred another spoonful of sugar into her mug, stirring forcefully enough to slosh coffee onto the countertop. "Yes, I have had a crappy few years, but so have you. The difference is I had help. Whenever I was struggling, I had you and my Mum and Dad and all the doctors and nurses rallying around to help me. You have done everything by yourself, in secret." Maya looked at her friend and shook her head sadly. "You are the strongest person I know, and I didn't even know it, you know?" She let out a snort of laughter. "I am such a selfish bitch" she said, looking Alice in the eye. "Can you forgive me?"

"There's nothing to forgive" Alice said, pouring herself another mug of coffee and helping herself to a banana from the fruit bowl. "How about I take Freddie with me and the kids to playgroup this morning and you get some sleep?"

Maya's face lit up. "That sounds fucking fantastic. I love you" said Maya throwing her arms around Alice. "I had better stop drinking this coffee" she said with a grin, "I don't want caffeine spoiling my nap."

The walk to the library for playgroup took much longer than Alice expected. Freddie and Lottie insisted on walking all the way and progress was painfully slow. Alice didn't mind. The two of them looked so sweet walking in front of the buggy, holding hands and chattering to each other as they toddled along. All her attention was on the children, so she didn't notice that they had walked right up to Maggie until it was too late. Lottie spotted her first and ran over to Maggie, wrapping her arms around her legs. "Lottie bear" laughed Maggie picking her up and giving her a hug. Lottie had her arms around Maggie's neck and was hugging her tightly. Alice was flustered. She knew she owed Maggie an explanation for leaving, but she was afraid to start a conversation she may not want to hear the answer to. "Look, about us leaving…" She began. Maggie put a hand up to stop her talking, shaking her head. "I get it, but let's not talk here," she said sadly, putting Lottie back down on her feet. "I miss you guys," she said as she turned to walk away. Alice stood, rooted to the spot. It had hurt more than she thought it would to see Maggie today. She had thought all she felt toward her was anger, but she realised she missed her too. Maggie had given her the courage to change her life and leave Ben. She had taught her that she could be strong and independent. She had thought Maggie loved her and the children as they had loved her. Her betrayal cut deep. Yet Alice realised she was not yet ready to cut her out of their lives completely. She may not want to be her friend right now, but she had to acknowledge what she had lost. "Maggie" she called, waiting for her to turn around. "I miss you too."

CHAPTER 27
MAGGIE 2018

Maggie arrived at the school a few minutes early to pick up Soraya. She took her place in the playground with the other mothers and listened to them chatting about the various details of their lives. She had not managed to make friends with any of them yet as they rarely spoke to anyone outside of their various cliques, but for now she was happy to stand in the sunshine enjoying her good mood. The bell rang and everyone looked toward the door where their children were being sent out. Soraya was often slow to leave, so Maggie was not concerned until all the children had left and she was still standing alone. Soraya's class teacher Miss Whitehead came to the door and beckoned for Maggie to approach. The teacher had a grave look on her face. "What's going on?" said Maggie, trying to look around the teacher to see if Soraya was behind her. Her brow furrowed as she fiddled nervously with her keys. "Is Soraya ok?"

"I need you to follow me please," said Miss Whitehead. "It will all be explained. Soraya is fine." She turned away from Maggie and walked into the building. Maggie had no choice but to follow. The woman's attitude was starting to annoy her. Why wouldn't she tell her what was going on? Her mind was churning, worrying that Soraya was hurt or injured or had done something horrible to another child. She had seemed so calm and happy this morning.

Maggie became more concerned as they headed toward the boardroom next to the head teacher's office. She could hear several voices speaking through the open door, but none of them was Soraya. The voices fell silent as she turned into the doorway. A quick scan of the room revealing Mr Matthews and two social workers that she recognised along with her own social worker Vivien. No-one smiled as she entered the room. "Ah, good afternoon Mrs ~Taylor" began Mr Matthews, "please take a seat." He motioned for her to sit opposite him. Everyone else in the room had taken their places either side of him, so when Maggie sat down, she had the impression that she was at an interview up against a panel of hostile interviewers. She sat as she had been asked, deciding to play it cool until she could work out what was going on. The room went silent. No one wanted to be the first to speak, and Maggie certainly wasn't going to make it easy for them by providing them with a conversation starter. Sensing the hostility in the room Maggie arranged her facial features into a neutral expression. She didn't want to give anything away until she knew exactly what she was up against. She took a seat near the door, subconsciously wanting to be aware of her exit route. "Ok, good afternoon everyone, let's get started" said Mr Matthews in a business-like manner, directing his speech toward Maggie. "Let me introduce everyone. Vivien you already know, these are David Sampson, Senior Social Worker and Jenny Pinkfield, Head of Children's Services. You should know that concerns have been raised and Mr Sampson is here to begin an investigation...."

"What concerns? Who has raised concerns?" said Maggie, moving forward to sit on the edge of her seat, hands on the table in front of her. She looked at Mr Matthews who refused to hold her gaze. Eventually, after a pause of what seemed like minutes but was probably a couple of seconds, the head social worker spoke up. He was a shrill sounding man, with sharp features that reminded Maggie of a rat. She stared at him as he spoke, unable to take in what he was saying. "Concerns were raised by Soraya's class teacher this morning. Soraya has been behaving erratically, and this morning she came into school obviously distressed and made a statement to the teacher that raised some red flags."

"No, that's not true." Maggie interrupted, feeling confused. "Soraya was fine this morning. She was in a lovely mood. She had pancakes..."

"....so the upshot of that is that all three children will be placed into protective care until a full investigation can take place." Continued Sampson. Maggie stared at him, slack jawed. "I'm sorry, could you please repeat that?" she said. "The children are in protective custody with us. I don't understand what you are telling me".

The social worker gave her a pitying look and spoke to her slowly, as he would to an infant.

"Unfortunately, Mrs Taylor. There is a question over Mr Taylor's relationship with the children. A very severe accusation has been made and I'm sure you understand that for the children's safety they have been removed from the household until we can investigate."

Maggie shook her head, "No I don't understand. It's not true. Daniel loves the children. He would never do anything to hurt them." She looked down at her hands on the table, trying to process what she had been told. "Is this because he raised his voice at her?" She looked up at the faces around the table who were watching her with a mixture of pity and disdain. "What exactly did she say? Can I speak to her? Where is she?" Sampson opened his mouth to speak, but Vivien put her hand up to stop him. "Maggie, I'm sure everything will be ok, but when a child makes an accusation, we have to take it seriously. I'm afraid in this situation we have to do an investigation to prove you innocent. And once it's over, everything can go back to normal." She moved around the table to take a seat next to Maggie. She placed her hand over Maggie's on the table, attempting to calm her down. Maggie shook her hand off and jumped up out of her seat, pacing up and down the small room. "You think that we can get back to normal after this?" she shook her head in disbelief. "You think Soraya can make an accusation, and we can be investigated, and everything can just go back to normal? That's not how life works" She took a breath, forcing herself to stay calm and not get angry, afraid that if she did it would give them reason to think that the accusations were true. "Is anyone going to tell me what she has accused him of?" She looked from person to person, finally fixing her gaze on Sampson. "Well?" she demanded. Sampson looked to each of the other adults in the room, then down at his notes, seeming to come to a decision. Speaking quietly he said "I shouldn't be telling you any of this, but I think it's only fair for you to know that Soraya has indicated that there have been inappropriate sexual advances made by your husband. She has described being touched intimately by him. She is speaking to an expert in child sexual assault cases, then she will be joining her brothers in a temporary foster placement."

Maggie slumped down in her chair. Tears welled in her eyes and slid slowly down her face. "Daniel is going to be devastated." She puffed out a breath, pulling herself together. "Do we need a lawyer or something?" she said. Trying to take stock of the situation. "What happens now?"

"Well," said Vivien, "We will need to speak to you and Daniel, separately of course. Soraya and the twins will be interviewed by an expert child psychologist and depending on what comes out of those interviews will determine the next steps."

Maggie nodded quietly. "So how long will all this take? When can the children come home?" Everyone looked toward Sampson for the answer. He gave a little shrug. "I don't know Mrs Taylor. These things are never quick."

"Right then" said Maggie, getting up and swinging her handbag onto her shoulder preparing to leave. "I need to go home and break the news to my husband that he is being accused of being a paedophile." She stared defiantly at each person in the room, business-like, allowing her eyes to rest on Sampson's. "I assume we are done here?" He nodded at her and she left the room, slamming the door behind her.

Maggie held it together until she reached the car. She sat behind the steering wheel, staring straight ahead, not knowing what to do. She should be going home to break the news to Daniel, but how was she supposed to tell him what had happened? The news would break him. On the other hand, if she didn't leave soon, he would start to worry. Either way, she had to go home in a few minutes to face the music. She desperately tried to think of a way of breaking this to Daniel that would not break him, but she came up blank. She allowed herself a few minutes to cry before angrily wiping away her tears and starting up the car to drive home.

As she had predicted Daniel was pacing in front of the window when she arrived home, worrying about her and the children as they were running late. His mind always seemed to jump to the worst-case scenario. He came out of the front door and opened the car door for her. "Where are the kids?" he said, a small V of concern appearing between his eyes. "Is everything ok?" Maggie got out of the car and without saying anything she stepped toward him and hugged him tightly. She could feel him trembling in her arms as she told him right there on the driveway, everything that had been said at the school. They walked arm in arm into the house and took a seat on the sofa in the lounge. Neither of them knew what to say, so they just sat there, hugging in silence, until the room was completely dark.

CHAPTER 28
ALICE 2019

It was starting to rain. Alice struggled to fit the rain cover over the buggy. She didn't want to wake Alfie, who had finally nodded off to sleep. He was teething and had kept her up all night. She had moved into the lounge with him, so she didn't wake Maya and the other two children and had fallen asleep eventually in the armchair. She had a sore neck this morning and combined with the sleep deprivation, it was leading to a foul mood. She finally hooked the last clip on the rain cover and continued into town. She had barely left the house for three weeks. Her issues with Ben and Maggie were playing on her mind. She felt as though she were on the edge of a panic attack all the time. Maya had convinced her that she needed to start getting out and about again, so she had agreed to do the supermarket shop today.

The rain was starting to come down harder and as Alice looked around for somewhere dry to wait, she spotted a friendly face waving at her from the coffee shop. She smiled at Oliver and headed toward him, turning round to drag the heavy buggy up the step into the shop. Oliver came over to greet her, giving her a kiss on the cheek and taking control of the buggy. He helped her manoeuvre the wieldy contraption into the corner where they could keep an eye on the sleeping children and waved down a waitress for Alice to place an order. "How are you?" Oliver finally said once they both had their drinks in front of them. "I haven't seen you since the Tearoom opened". He stirred two sugars into his latte and gave her a friendly smile. "That seems so long ago now" sighed Alice. "So much has happened since then. Did you hear about Maggie and her secret past?" Christian was intrigued. "No, that sounds all very mysterious" he laughed. Alice frowned slightly, two small lines appearing at the bridge of her nose. "It is mysterious, but not in a good way. She was married, until about a year ago when her husband topped himself." She looked at Oliver to see how he was reacting. His eyes were round, and his mouth formed a little O of surprise. "Apparently," She continued "he was being done for abusing one of their foster children, and the shame of it was too much for him. As soon as he died Maggie ran away and came to live here. Probably trying to find somewhere no one knows her." She took a sip of her drink and gazed at her children. Silently thankful that she had found out about Maggie's past before something could happen to them. "Well, now her secret is out, and I have no-where to live. So, me and my two precious babies are staying with Maya for a while. Just until I can work out what to do." Oliver frowned. "Why are you staying at Maya's? What happened to Ben?" Alice fiddled with the empty sugar packets on the table, her cheeks flushed. "Ben and I are no longer together. The truth is, he was aggressive and violent toward me." She looked up at Oliver through her fringe, trying to gauge his reaction. She knew she should not feel embarrassed, but she had tried so hard to make it seem as though she had a perfect life and a beautiful, loving family, that it was harder than she imagined to admit the truth. "Go on" said Oliver, encouragingly. "There's not that much to tell really" said Alice in a small voice. "It's the same story you hear on TV and in books all the time. He was jealous and controlling. He didn't like me going out and meeting other people. Then one day a few weeks ago it all went too far. We had a big row; he took things too far and I ran away with the children in the middle of the night." She took a gulp of her drink. Oliver was looking at her with a mixture of pity and anger. "I'm so sorry Alice. I had no idea..." Alice put her hand on his arm and shook her head bleakly, "You had no way of knowing. That's the point. It was all secret. No one knew. And he somehow convinced me that no one would care or want to help me." She shook her head and looked at her children again. "Looking back, I can't believe that was me. He totally had me convinced that I was helpless." Christian put his arm around her, and she leaned her head on his shoulder. They sat in silence like that for a couple of minutes, lost in their own thoughts.

The sound of a fist banging on the window beside them made them both jump. Standing in front of them, rage written in his every feature, was Ben. "Whore" he shouted, loud enough to make everyone in the coffee shop look in their direction. "Fucking slut." Alice gasped and shrank back in her seat. Oliver put out a reassuring hand to her. "It's ok, you're safe. He's not going to do anything here." He stood protectively beside her, waiting to see what Ben was going to do next. Lottie woke up and seeing her Dad in a rage outside the window she screamed and struggled out of the buggy and into her mum's arms. The scream woke Alfie, who added to the noise with wails of protest. Ben was glaring at them through the window. Alice was paralysed. She hugged Lottie close to her and reached out her free arm for Alfie as Oliver unbuckled him from the buggy and handed him to her.

Ben banged on the window again and screamed something unintelligible at them, which made Alice and Lottie flinch with terror. That was enough for Oliver. He pushed past the buggy and propelled himself out of the door toward Ben. Without saying a word, he squared up to Ben and punched him full in the face. Ben crumpled to the floor in a heap. Oliver shook his hand, causing tiny droplets of blood to fly off and hit the window. Ben was out cold on the pavement. Oliver walked back into the café to a smattering of applause from the patrons nearest them who had seen the whole incident.

Oliver sat back down and looked at Alice with a sheepish grin. "Erm, I'm not sure what I should say now" he laughed. "That blokes a bit of a prick". Alice smiled, wiping tears from Lottie's face with a wet wipe. "Yes, I have to agree". A waitress approached him with a wet tea towel full of ice to place on his swollen fingers along with three slices of cake which she told them was on the house. "That was awesome" she winked at Oliver as she took their used cups away.

Outside on the pavement Ben had woken up and was leaning against the glass of the window rubbing his jaw. Alice stood up and made her way to the exit. "Watch the kids a minute" she instructed Oliver, who nodded and directed Lottie's attention to the chocolate cake in front of her. Alice approached her husband and looked down at him in disdain. How had she ever been afraid of this pathetic excuse for a human? He looked up at her, one eye was starting to swell shut and he had the start of a large purple bruise spreading across his face. Let him explain that to his customers and the girls he flirted with in his office. "I'm not scared of you anymore Ben, you pathetic little man. You will never bully me ever again. I'm getting a divorce." As she turned to walk away from him Ben shouted at her, his voice slurred from the punch and the alcohol he had obviously enjoyed with his lunch. "Go back to your boyfriend you stupid bitch. I don't want you anyway." Alice stopped walking and clenched her fists. What she wanted to do was turn around and kick him in the face, but she would never do that in front of her kids. That would make her as bad as him. She crouched down and looked him straight in the eye. "Everyone in this town is going to know what a despicable man you are. If you ever come near me or my kids again you are going to regret it." With that she stood and walked away from him, leaving him on the floor with a look of surprise and defeat on his bruised and bloody face...

CHAPTER 29
MAGGIE 2018

Maggie awoke to the sound of something smashing against the front door. She checked the clock. 3am. Daniel was still sleeping so she slipped quietly out of bed and padded down the hallway to peer out of the window overlooking the front of the house. She couldn't see anything untoward, so she continued down the stairs. Before she got even halfway down, she could tell what had made the noise. Eggs had been thrown at the glass of the front door and had left streaky lines all the way to the floor as they had dripped down. Maggie knew from experience that the best time to remove the egg was when it was still wet. If she waited until morning when it was dry it would be ten times harder to clean up. There was no way she could leave the egg there for Daniel to see in the morning. His mental health had plummeted since the accusation had been made and she didn't think he could cope with this latest humiliation.

Maggie filled up a bucket with hot soapy water and took the mop out to the front of the house with her. She had a quick look up and down the road to make sure she was alone before swiftly cleaning the sticky mess from the door. It had been three months since the children had been taken from them and life had become almost unbearable. The first time she had been targeted Maggie had been terrified. She had gone to the supermarket to do the weekly shop. She walked around the store with her head down, careful not to catch anyone's eye. The cashier at the till had recognised her and attempted to engage her in conversation, but Maggie had shut her down as quickly as she could, afraid that others nearby would hear and be able to identify her. Obviously, she was more recognisable that she thought, as when she returned to her car it had been covered in red paint. The shock hit her full in the chest as she stepped out of the supermarket into the car park. Her little car sat all alone in an island of red paint that has pooled around the vehicle. Not looking around to see if anyone was watching she opened the door using a spare carrier bag as a glove to avoid touching the sticky handle. She threw the bags of shopping into the boot and drove away as quickly as she could. She held on to her tears until she pulled up on the driveway where the relief of making it back home overwhelmed her. By the time she had hauled the crushed and battered shopping into the house she was crying in full flow and was almost hysterical. That was the last time either of them had been shopping. The attacks to the house had slowed recently. Maggie assumed people were getting bored. Other stories had taken over from theirs as the source of local gossip. This was a setback that they could do without.

Once Maggie had finished clearing up the eggy mess, she sat in the lounge with a cup of coffee. There was no way she was going to be able to fall asleep now. She picked up the laptop that lay on top of a box of electronic equipment that had recently been returned to them. The police had taken their phones, pc, tablets, and laptops, presumably to look for evidence of child abuse or porn. Daniel had shown no interest in setting up his pc again to start working. Maybe they needed a holiday. A little break away from this town might help get Daniel back on his feet. Maggie searched for holidays in the sun for a couple of hours. She found a perfect little villa with a pool in the middle of nowhere in Italy with its own orchard and orange grove. Maybe a few weeks out there, where no one knew them, would do them the world of good. And by the time they got back this would all have blown over in everyone's minds and life could return to normal. As soon as Maggie heard Daniel moving around, she made up a cafetiere of coffee and toasted a couple of croissants. She took them up to him in bed and opened the laptop with the picture of the villa splashed across the screen. He barely acknowledged her as she sat on the side of the bed nearest him and told him about the features of the house. "Daniel, will you just look at it please?" she implored. "I can't stand to see you so down like this. Let's go away for a while, somewhere quiet where no one knows us." Daniel rolled his eyes and helped himself to a cup of coffee. "Are you not going to say anything?" Maggie continued "don't you think it looks beautiful?" she scrolled the screen across to show him the orange grove and the idyllic placement of the pool looking out over the lush, green hills. "yeah, it's great" he said around a mouthful of croissant, his eyes barely flicking to the screen. "You are not even looking" said Maggie, in exasperation. She shut the lid of the laptop firmly and flung it toward the bottom of the bed. "how are you gonna get there? Eh?" said Daniel, suddenly angry. "are we going to teleport there?" He was sitting up in bed now, staring at her with angry eyes. "no. We will have to get a taxi to the airport, then wait in line with a whole load of people, then at the other end we will get on a bus full of yet more people to get to the villa. Any one of those hundreds of people could recognise us, then there we are in the middle of a mob of angry people who think we are fucking paedos" He stood up, pulling the dressing gown around himself, red faced and shouting now. "So no, I don't want to go on fucking holiday". He stormed into the bathroom and slammed the door, leaving Maggie on the edge of the bed white faced and teary.

A few days after the accusation Maggie had gone into work and had been summoned to the head teacher's office. When she got there, she was met by the Human Resources person and the Chair of Governors. Before they even had a chance to speak, Maggie knew they would ask her to step down from her position. They told her they had to put her on suspension until the investigation into her and her husband had been completed. Maggie didn't want to get into an argument with them, so she calmly accepted what they had to say and walked out of the building without talking to another soul. Daniel had been surprised to see her when she walked back into the house that morning. She opened the front door and walked straight into his arms as he sat at the table in the lounge/diner. He didn't say anything, just let her cry on his shoulder until there were no more tears left. He had not left the house at all for the past three days and had barely managed to shower or eat. Once Maggie had cried herself out, she walked numbly up the stairs to prepare lunch. Her only focus now was to make sure that Daniel was ok. He was already seriously depressed, and it was starting to worry her. She wondered how bad things had to get before she should call in professional help. At the moment she was working on the assumption that all the time he was getting dressed and eating, they had not achieved that position yet.

The investigators had already spoken to them both alone and together more than once, going over and over the same old questions.

Within the week the local newspaper had found out about the story and posted information about them on their website. That was when the abuse had started. At first there were whispered comments in the streets as they walked by, or a whispered comment behind their back. Daniel's work dried up and his depression took a turn for the worse. He gave up showering and shaving completely and spent most of his time watching DVDs. He couldn't bear to even watch TV or use the internet in case he heard about himself or other child abuse stories that would set him off again. Maggie didn't know why the investigation was taking so long. They were innocent. Surely it should be quite a quick process to clear up this mistake. After two months Maggie was starting to fall into depression along with Daniel. She had lost contact with all of her friends from work, and had stopped looking at social media, afraid of the name calling and trolling that was now an everyday occurrence. None of her friends wanted to be seen contacting her either in real life or online, so she quickly became isolated and miserable. Their social worker, Vivien, who originally had been 100% on their side and had been a constant source of optimism, had stopped visiting the house, and was not answering her mobile. There was no point trying to argue with these people. They were not interested in listening to reason. She was glad that she had the money she had inherited from her foster parents. Without that Maggie didn't know how they would have coped. Neither of them had worked for three months.

CHAPTER 30
MAYA 2019

Maya placed a tray loaded with chicken soup and orange juice in front of her mum. "Please try and eat something. You look like shit." She handed Pamela the spoon and took a seat next to the bed. "Do you need a doctor?" Pamela shook her head and blew on a spoonful of soup to cool it. "I'm fine. You don't need to make such a fuss."

"Actually, I'm not the one making a fuss. Dad called, said you were ill and losing weight. So I am just here to be the food police."

"He's over-reacting. I have a touch of the stomach flu, that's all." Pamela sighed, picking up the spoon. "How's my precious little Grandbaby?"

"He's good. Playing in the garden with Dad. He's determined to turn him into a sports freak. I swear, since he recovered all he ever talks about is football and cricket" She laughed and stood to watch them out of the window, kicking a ball around the garden. "I will bring him up to see you as soon as we know you are not contagious. Still can't risk it yet."

Pamela nodded. "If I still feel like this at the end of the week, I will call the doctor. I promise" Maya sat down in the armchair next to the bed. "I need you to feel better for next week because we are going to the hospital on Saturday to present the cheque for the Children's Cancer Ward. We are guests of honour at their charity fundraiser ball." She grinned at her mum. "Can you believe we raised £25k Mum? That's pretty frickin' huge"

Pamela glanced up to the ceiling, her forehead creased. "I need to tell you something." She took a deep breath, her eyes fixed on her hands, avoiding looking at Maya. "About that big donation." She bit her lip. "The seventeen thousand pounds came from Maggie Taylor." Maya furrowed her brow and searched her mother's face. "Why would she do that?" she asked. "And why not tell me? I don't understand. What am I missing here?"

"Before I met your Dad, I was in a relationship with guy for two years. I thought he was the one, my first love." Pamela glanced at Maya to check she was listening. Maya nodded for her to continue. "We had done some travelling together, backpacking around Europe, paying our way by picking fruit and tending bar. We were at home for Christmas, seeing our families and I started getting sick in the mornings. Well, of course, I was pregnant" She looked to the ceiling, lost in her memories. "I called him at his parent's house and told him the news, and basically that was the last I saw of him. The day we were supposed to leave for France he called me to say he had a job with his Dad that was starting in Scotland and he didn't want to be with me anymore." Pamela wiped away a tear, surprised at how much it hurt to think about this, so many years later. Maya pulled the chair closer to the bed and held her Mother's hand. "I didn't see him again. And I was pregnant and alone. I went back to live with my parents and as soon as the baby was born, I had her adopted." Pamela watched Maya's face as what she was saying finally dawned on her. She carried on talking, not giving Maya a chance to ask questions. "I met your father not long after that, and the rest you know." Pamela looked up at Maya, trying to read her daughter's face. Maya sat back in the chair, silently looking around the room for a minute or two, thinking over all she had been told.

"So, I have a half-sister." She said thoughtfully. "Maggie is my half-sister." She nodded to herself. "How long have you known she was your child?" She looked at her mum blankly. Pam dropped her eyes to the floor. Maya had a moment of realisation. "You knew before she came here didn't you?" She stated, not bothering to wait for an answer. "You knew the whole time. You knew she was the one who made the donation. That's why you tried to get me to refuse it. To keep your dirty little secret."

Pamela was crying silently now. Maya stood and looked out of the window once again. "Does Dad know?" She asked quietly. Pamela dabbed at her eyes with a tissue and sniffed loudly. "He didn't know anything until I told him this morning. He didn't know any of it," she sighed. Maya slumped back down into the chair. "So, all that stuff about Maggie's husband being a paedophile. Is that all true? Or were you just trying to get me to stay away from her?" She stood again and began pacing in the small room, not aware of what she was doing, but unable to keep still. "All this time I have been friends with her, and enemies with her, tearing myself up over her, and you have known the whole time that she was my sister" Maya was almost shouting now. Hurt giving way to anger. "I have had a sister my whole fucking life, and I knew nothing about her. I have gone through everything alone, wishing I had a sibling to share my life with and you knew that I did, and never bloody told me." Maya shook her head again in disbelief, thinking over all the times in her life that she had yearned to have a brother or sister to help her through or to celebrate with. She sat back down on the arm of the chair and handed a tissue to her mother, who was crying steadily and silently. "Does Maggie know who I am? Does she know she's an Aunty?" she asked, almost afraid of the answer.

CHAPTER 31
MAGGIE 2018

"Are you nearly ready Danny?" called Maggie from the front door. "We are going to be late". He had got into the shower after her more than 30 minutes ago. He should be ready by now. She checked her make up in the hall mirror and grabbed a tissue from the box on the windowsill to wipe off her lipstick. She and Daniel were due to attend a review meeting with the police and social workers and she was worrying about how she should look. The lipstick made her look less 'motherly' she thought, so it had to go. She checked her watch again. There was still no sign of Daniel coming down any time soon, so she ran back up the stairs to hurry him along. She turned the corner into the bedroom to find him sliding under the covers. "No, no, no, no," She said, rushing across the room to pull the duvet off him. "You have to come to this Danny. How will it look if you aren't there?" Daniel shrugged and pulled the duvet back up to his chest. "I don't care anymore. They never listen to me anyway. They will decide whatever they decide, with or without me in the room." He picked up the remote control and switched the tv on to a home makeover channel. Maggie could barely make herself heard over the sound of sawing from the TV. "Please Danny. I know you hate this, and you are probably right, but I need you there." Maggie spoke as calmly as she could, however she could barely suppress the bubble of panic rising rapidly to her chest. "What am I supposed to tell them?" She sat on the edge of the bed and took the remote from him, switching the tv off. "I don't care what you tell them." Danny said, snatching the remote back and clicking the tv on again. "It doesn't matter either way." He settled back against the pillows, staring blankly at the glowing TV screen.

Maggie watched him silently for a second, before shaking her head and taking a deep breath. She looked at her watch. "Sorry Danny, but I need to go now. Keep your phone near you, I will let you know what they say" she said, giving up the fight. She leant over and kissing him on the forehead. "I love you Danny. No matter what happens next I will always love you." Daniel didn't respond. Maggie picked up her bag and hurried out to her car.

It was a short drive to the review meeting venue, which had been scheduled in the local police station. Maggie couldn't help but think this was a bad sign, but her lawyer had informed her that the police station was often the venue for these smaller meetings, purely because it had a large boardroom that was underused. Arriving at the station Maggie was met by the expensive lawyer that she had avoided speaking to until just over a month ago. She had to admit, he did a fantastic job. He had found several witnesses and evidentiary anomalies that had almost led to the case being thrown out. Maggie was not going to rest easy until the judge had declared her and Daniel completely innocent.

They walked together into the lobby to find that they were the last to arrive, so they moved swiftly into the boardroom to take their seats. The independent meeting chairperson sat at the head of the table and went through the usual pre meeting waffle, pointing out fire doors and water bottles. Maggie tuned out and tried to calm her mind, which was cycling through numerous different outcomes. She didn't dare to hope that anything good was going to happen.

"Good Afternoon, Ladies and Gentlemen," said the Chairperson, a handsome, stately woman that Maggie aged somewhere in her mid to late 50s. "As you all know, we are all here to investigate an allegation of a sexual nature against Mr Daniel Taylor by a looked after child in his care on 20th August this year." Maggie glanced sideways out of the corner of her eye, trying not to catch the eye of any of their accusers. She was happy to find that Soraya was not there. Maybe she would be giving her evidence by video link later in the proceedings. "Both Mr and Mrs Taylor have been thoroughly investigated by social services and the police, and character witnesses have been sought from among their friends and work colleagues, as well as from the school and childminding service that the children have been attending. All the children were found to be in good health and were seen to be thriving in this placement." Maggie sat totally still on her chair, listening to the summary of events. Heard as a list like this they sounded fairly innocuous, there was no hint of the soul crushing doubt and depression that had befallen Daniel or the stress and humiliation that both of them had suffered in losing their jobs and friends and the respect of their local community. She wanted to cry or shout out or simply to stand up and scream at the top of her lungs, to tell everyone how negative and harrowing this whole situation had been for her, but all she could do was sit quietly, with her hands folded on her lap, working to maintain a neutral expression on her face.

"It is our duty of care to make sure that any accusation levelled by a child is taken seriously and investigated thoroughly, with the assistance of the police if necessary. In this instance, I have reviewed all of the paperwork, copies of which are in the packs in front of you, and have to conclude that mistakes have been made, which have caused undue stress to Mr and Mrs Taylor, and for which I can only apologise." Maggie's head snapped up at this and she held the gaze of the chairperson, who was looking at her with compassion in her eyes.

"It has come to my attention that Soraya has retracted her allegation during an interview with her social worker and that has been backed up by statements made to a child psychologist. It seems that this was a false allegation, and as such, all charges of abuse are dropped." Maggie's mouth dropped open and tears pricked the back of her eyes. The chairperson took off her reading glasses and let them hang on the chain around her neck. In a less formal manner she spoke directly to Maggie. "Mrs Taylor, I am so sorry for everything that you have been put through during recent months. Not only has Soraya's accusation been found to be a total fabrication, but on review of her records of previous placements it was found that she has a history of making accusations of this nature. There is no way this situation should ever have escalated to this point. Please pass on my very sincere apologies to your husband." She closed her notebooks, picked up her pen and handbag and proceeded to leave the room. There was a buzz of conversation around the table, but Maggie sat dead still, unable to process what she had just heard until her lawyer reached over, placed a hand on hers and said "It's over Maggie. You can go home and tell Daniel it's all over." Maggie looked at her and seeing the relaxed smile on her face convinced her that what she thought she had heard was true. She allowed a small smile to turn up the corners of her mouth.

As Maggie was gathering her belongings to leave and preparing to text Daniel to let him know the good news, she was approached by her social worker who sat on the table, facing her. "So, Maggie," she said in a sickly-sweet voice, "We should make arrangements for the children moving back home." Maggie looked at her, incredulous. She opened and closed her mouth silently a couple of times before the utter rage that she had felt since August 20th came spilling out of her "Firstly, you don't get to call me Maggie," she said dangerously "Only my friends call me Maggie, and you most certainly are not my friend. Your incompetence nearly ruined me, my husband, and my marriage, so to you, I am Mrs Taylor. You may not call me Maggie." Everyone in the room was staring in their direction now, but Maggie was in full flow and didn't think she would be able to stop now even if she wanted to. "Secondly, our house stopped being home to those children the second that Soraya accused my husband of raping her. He can never feel safe in that house again with her or any other child in it, so we will not be arranging for anyone to come back to the house. We are done. "With that she swept out of the room and almost ran back to the car. Once she was safely out of sight of everyone Maggie dropped her head onto her hands on the steering wheel and sobbed.

Maggie didn't know how long she had been crying, but the sky had got considerably darker since she left the police station. She pulled out her mobile to check if Daniel had texted her. He hadn't, but she had not really expected him to. She could count on one hand the number of messages she had received from him in the past three months. Hopefully now they would be able to rebuild their lives and get back to being the happy couple that they once were. She made a mental note to ask her lawyer to contact the local paper and make sure they printed a retraction to their awful child abuse story that had turned the whole town against them. Her lawyer had suggested previously that they had a good case if they wanted to sue. There was no way that information about an allegation of this manner should have been known by anyone other than those involved, as no charges had been made. And now they had received a formal apology they could probably sue the investigators for failing to report Soraya rescinding her allegation. Not to mention the fact that they had never been warned about her history of allegations in the past. Maggie wondered to herself if they would have refused to take Soraya and the twins in if they had known her history. She liked to think that they wouldn't have. When all was said and done, there were positive aspects to fostering the children that she would always be grateful for. For a few short months they had been a happy family, and she couldn't regret that, no matter what had happened afterward.

As Maggie pulled up to the house, she was surprised to find that the lights were still off. It was almost 6.30pm, surely Daniel couldn't still be in bed, could he? She pressed the button on the garage zapper, but the door didn't open. She bashed the remote with her hand, wondering if the batteries were dying and pressed the button again. Nothing. She parked the car in front of the garage door and got out to open the door manually. She could hear Daniel's car engine running inside, which was odd. She assumed he was doing a service on it and banged on the door for him to let her in. She couldn't get the door open and he didn't hear her knocking and calling so she went inside the house to access the garage from the internal door.

As soon as she walked in through the front door, Maggie sensed that something was wrong. None of the lights were on, even though it was now almost completely dark. The door to the garage was slightly ajar and the smell of petrol and exhaust fumes was strong in the hallway. She flicked on the light and covered her mouth with her scarf, pushing open the garage door and stepping in. The light from the hall illuminated a square on the front windscreen of the car. Inside she could see Adam slumped over in the driver's seat as though he were sleeping. She took another step into the garage and flicked the light switch. Her attention was drawn immediately to the piece of hosepipe that was wedged in the cracked open window of the car, filling the cockpit with deadly carbon monoxide. Moving as quickly as she could Maggie pushed past the car and opened the garage door, letting in fresh air. She could already feel a headache pounding at her temples from the poisonous air. She opened the driver's door, turned off the engine and fumbled with Daniel's seatbelt. She could hear herself crying "No, no, no, no," over and over, but couldn't stop herself. She managed to drag Daniel out of the seat and pulled him by his shoulders until his face was near the open door. "Somebody help me" she screamed into the street as loudly as she could, whilst franticly feeling Daniel's neck for a pulse. "Somebody help. Call an ambulance" she screamed again. She started CPR, giving Daniel her breath, and doing chest compressions the way she had been shown in her first aid course for becoming a foster carer. Now that Daniel was in the light, she could see that his skin was cherry red. She knew that was a bad sign, but she carried on doing compressions and breathing for him until she saw a dog walker turn into the street. "Help, help me" she screamed toward them. The dog walker heard her and came running. "Call an ambulance" she instructed him breathlessly. Doing chest compressions was harder than she realised, and she was starting to tire. She heard the dog walker get through to the emergency services. He handed her the phone and indicated that he would take over CPR while she spoke to them. Within minutes the ambulance was on the scene, followed swiftly by a police car.

The paramedics took over from Maggie and the dog walker, whose name was Donald. A female police officer took them to one side and started asking questions. Maggie could only half hear what she was being asked. Her eyes were glued to what was happening with her husband. He was now hooked up to a drip and a bag was breathing for him. He had been shocked several times and they were still doing chest compressions, but she could see they were close to giving up. She put her hand up to stop the policewoman asking her any more questions and moved as if to go back to Daniel's side. "I don't' think that's a good idea Mrs Taylor," said the police officer "let the paramedics do their job". Maggie ignored her and walked blindly toward her husband. Tears falling freely down her cheeks. She fell on her knees beside him on the gravel drive just as the paramedic pronounced him dead. She brushed his hair away from his face as one of the medics removed the bag and tube from his mouth. He looked peaceful. As though he had slept through everything that had just happened. She felt someone place a blanket around her shoulders as she knelt on the ground and take an elbow to help her up. "No, leave me," she said, shaking off the helping hands. "I need to say goodbye." Maggie leant over and laid her head down on her husband's chest and sobbed quietly while everyone stood back to allow her a moment of privacy. She sat up when she heard a voice say, "I've found a note."

"What note?" she said, to no one in particular. "What note? I need to see the note. It's for me" she said, getting more anxious.

She stood up and a young police officer handed her a folded piece of paper that had the word Maggie written on it in purple ink. She allowed the police officer to guide her into the lounge and sit her down on the sofa with a cup of sweet tea. Maggie was holding the note in both hands, staring blankly at it and rocking slightly back and forth as she sat. She was simultaneously scared and desperate to open the letter, the two impulses fighting against each other causing her to freeze. The policewoman sat next to her on the sofa and placed one hand over hers. "Let me" she said, easing the note out of Maggie's grip and opening it up carefully. She read it aloud. "My dearest Maggie, please don't hate me for being the coward that I am. I can't go on like this anymore. The shame I have brought to our door is too much to bear. Please know I didn't do and would never do anything to hurt Soraya or anyone else. I loved those children as if they were our own, our sweet little perfect family. I have loved you since the moment I first saw you and I will continue loving you until the end of time. Forget about me. Go and live your life and be happy. I love you forever, your dearest Danny"

CHAPTER 32
ALICE 2019

Alice looked at the clock for the hundredth time that night. It was almost dawn and she had not yet managed to fall asleep. Her conversation with Maggie had been playing on her mind since she had spoken to her last week. She had been rash to move out and take the children without giving Maggie a chance to give her side of the story. She would expect someone to give her a chance in a similar situation. There could be an explanation for what had happened. And after all, Maggie was clearly not with her husband anymore and she wasn't in prison, so maybe everything had sorted itself out. She had trusted Maggie when she met her, and usually her instincts were good. She should learn to trust her gut. Maggie had helped her get away from Ben. She had never complained or said it was too hard or too big for her to do. She had seen a need and helped with it. And that was when Alice had still been pretty much a stranger to her.

She made a decision. Alice got up from the bed, avoiding waking the children, and dressed quickly. She slipped into the lounge and wrote a note for Maya in case the children woke. She took Maya's car keys from the bowl by the door and left.

There was the slightest glimmer of light on the horizon as Alice arrived at Maggie's flat. She climbed the stairs quickly, eager now to get this over with. She had her keys with her, but didn't want to scare Maggie by letting herself in. She knocked on the door and backed it up by sending a text. She waited a couple of minutes, peering in through a gap in the curtain on the door.

Maggie opened the door wearing a dressing gown and slippers. Her hair was all over the place, indicating that she had been tossing and turning all night herself. She opened the door, looking worried. "What is it?" she said quickly as she opened the door. "Is it the kids?"

"No, no, it's nothing like that" said Alice quickly, grabbing both of Maggie's hands to reassure her. "It's me. I need to apologize. I need to speak to you about..."

"It's ok. Calm down, take a breath" said Maggie. "Come in, I will make us a cup of tea"

The two of them drank tea and talked until the sun had risen and light was sparkling off the river below. Maggie explained everything that had happened with Daniel, right up to the moment she had moved to the town. "I'm so sorry I didn't tell you before Alice. I just thought I could leave and start again. I never meant to hurt you or the children." Her voice cracked as she tried to control her emotions. "All forgiven. Let's just put it behind us" said Alice, pulling Maggie in for a hug. Maggie pulled away and held Alice at arm's length. "There's something else. And as we are being honest, I really need to tell you." She closed her eyes, speaking quickly. "Maya is my half-sister. I was adopted at birth. I came here, to this town, to meet her." She opened her eyes slowly, scared that she had pushed Alice away again. Alice was smiling at her. "Well, that explains a lot" she laughed. "I mean, I had my theories, but I thought you either had a crush on her or were a stalker or something. This makes way more sense." Maggie shook her head "I'm such an idiot" she laughed.

Later that morning, Alice packed up all her things and moved herself and the children back into the flat with Maggie. Lottie was beside herself with excitement to be back with Maggie. Even Alfie seemed to pick up on the mood and was more smiley than usual. Once everything was all unpacked and the children were happily playing with Play-doh at the table Maggie handed Alice a cup of tea and sat opposite her. "I'm glad you are back

Alice" she smiled. "In fact, there is something I wanted to ask you." Alice was intrigued. "Ok, what is it?" she raised her eyebrows in question.

"Well, the tea shop is doing well, and getting really busy, which is great and everything," said Maggie, putting her cup down and reaching over to help Lottie remove a sticky lump of dough from the table top, "but it's too much for me to handle by myself." She looked hopefully at Alice. "I was wondering if you would be interested in being my business partner?" Alice stared at Maggie, her mouth slightly open. A tear rolled gently down her cheek. Maggie took her hand. "It's ok if you don't want to." She said quickly. "It's too much for you with the kids and everything. I'm sorry I was being insensitive..." Alice put a hand up to stop Maggie talking. "No, it's not that.... It's just, no-one has ever had that much faith in me. I'm stunned." She wiped her eyes, a huge grin brightening her face. "I would love to work with you. I can't think of anything I would like to do more."

Before she had even finished speaking Maggie had jumped out of her chair and run around the table to envelop Alice in a hug. She broke away quickly, grabbing a notepad from the counter and flipping it open on the table. "Right, we have plans to make, this is going to be so good... and don't worry about childcare or anything like that, we can take it in turns to look after them." Alice sat back in the chair watching her friend in wonder. How much her life had changed in just 12 short months. For the first time in as long as she could remember she felt hopeful about the future.

CHAPTER 33
MAYA 2019

Maya put her hands on her knees and took a deep breath. Right up until this moment she had been determined and even excited about what she was going to do, but now standing at his front door with her hand poised over the doorbell she had come over feeling dizzy and faint. "You can do this," she told herself out loud as she stood upright once more. Again, she raised her hand to press the doorbell but didn't make it. She leaned her head back and shook her golden hair out then rolled her head around on her neck as if preparing for a boxing match. Maya lifted her hand for a third time, but this time the decision was made for her and the door opened.

"Maya, hi," said a familiar voice that soothed her thrumming nerves, like honey. "Is everything ok?" he said, trying to work out why she was there on the doorstep and why she looked so on edge. He stopped back, opening the door wide to let her in. Maya stepped across the threshold and carried on down the hall to the kitchen. She would feel far more comfortable having this conversation with a cup of tea in her hand. "Hi" she started in rather a brusque manner. "No, everything's not ok. Well, it is, but there have been secrets; and I can't keep things secret anymore. I won't keep things secret anymore." She filled the kettle absently while she spoke and flicked it on. She was aware that nothing was making sense, but now she had started speaking she just couldn't find a way to stop. "My Mum is going to die. She has Cancer, and she is going to die, and she thought she could do the whole fucking thing without telling anyone. A while ago

I would have thought that was fine, you know, you do you and all that, but then I found out I had a sister I didn't know about and I have missed out on for 21 years, and I realised that it's just too unfair you know? All that time I have lost." She poured hot water into two coffee mugs, not pausing long enough for an answer. "And I realised who am I to bitch about that when I am doing the exact same thing. So, I know this is probably not something you want to hear, and it may be complicated because you had a wife at the time, but I think you have a right to know and Freddie has a right to know who his Father is. And you don't have to do anything about it or anything, because honestly we have done fine for the past three years, but just in case you want to know, and just in case Freddie ever wants to know who his Dad is, I think you should know that it's you." Maya took a breath then, sitting down and placing two hot cups of tea on the kitchen table. She breathed a sigh of relief. The speech had not gone as smoothly as it had done the several times she had rehearsed it in her head, but it had felt good to get it out there. She was met with stony silence, so she thought she ought to recap the important point. In a calmer voice she said "I know this is a big shock, but you are a Dad. Freddie is your son."

Maya made no attempt to drink her tea. She was watching Oliver intently. He looked confused and surprised at first, but his expression soon mellowed and morphed into something approaching joy. When he still hadn't said a single word after almost four minutes of waiting Maya interrupted his thought process. "Well?" she demanded. "you've got to say something. I've laid my shit out in front of you here. You can't keep me hanging." Oliver stared at her open mouthed. "Only you Maya Young, would march into someone's house, drop a bomb on them, then complain that *they* are making *you* feel uncomfortable." He let out a hysterical little laugh. Maya couldn't help but join in. Soon the two of them were holding their sides and panting for breath. Finally, Oliver calmed himself enough to speak. "Maya, I think it's amazing that I am a Dad. You know I have always cared about Freddie. I did even wonder at one point if he might possibly be mine, but you cut me out of your life so thoroughly I didn't get the chance to speak to you about it."

"I had to cut you out," said Maya, "I loved you Oliver. I loved you so completely that I was sure that if people saw the way I looked at you that they would guess you were the father right away. So, I forced myself never to look at you. Then after a while it became difficult to even be in the same room as you. I'm sorry you had to think that was hate, but the only way I could keep my secret was to push you away." She dropped her eyes to the floor and wiped away a tear. Oliver appeared to be lost in memories, thinking about the previous three years during which he and Maya had barely managed to maintain eye contact, let alone have a conversation. He had thought she hated him. Now he thought that maybe she should have, having had to struggle with a sick child when she was only 17 and still not much more than a child herself. Maya looked at him. Deadly serious now. "I cut you out of my life because all the while you were still with your wife, I couldn't bear to see you every day and know that you couldn't be with me. I couldn't tell you about Freddie because that would have put you in a horrible position. There was no way you could leave Jane while she had cancer but if you knew I was pregnant you would have wanted to do the right thing and help me. I couldn't put you in that situation. And then when Jane died, I couldn't be that woman who appears as soon as the wife is out of the picture. People would hate me." She glanced up at Oliver and was surprised to find he was crying. She closed her eyes tightly and carried on speaking, afraid she would chicken out if she stopped now and it would forever remain unsaid. "And, just in case you are wondering if I might have made a mistake, I know that Freddie is yours because I have never been with anyone else." She paused, looking into Oliver's steely grey eyes. "The truth is, I love you Oliver, and I always have. And if you don't love me back, well that's fine too because you never asked for any of this. But if you would like to be part of Freddie's family and mine, you would make us both very happy" A tear ran down Maya's cheek, snaking down her neck. Oliver stood and wrapped his arms around her, hugging her tightly for a full minute. He then stood an arm's length from her and took both her hands in his. He had a contented smile on his face as his whispered "I'm a Dad" repeating it over and over until the two of them were jumping around the kitchen together. When they stopped Maya leaned in to give Oliver a kiss of the cheek.

"Do you want to come and meet you son?"

CHAPTER 34 MAGGIE MAYA 2019

It was an unseasonably warm day. The weather forecast said they were in the grip of an Indian Summer. Maggie took advantage of the Autumn sunshine to open the doors to the tearoom terrace and put cushions out on the chairs so guests could sit outside and watch the boats and the swans floating by. She had received a cryptic message from Maya asking her to reserve a big, family table for a special occasion, which she had done. She made an extra effort to make it look nice, putting out the best tablecloth and tea service as well as jugs of handtied flower bouquets and candles, assuming it was for a birthday or similar celebration.

Maggie was busy folding linen napkins into the shape of roses when Alice walked into the tearoom with Lottie and Alfie. "Hi, she waved across the room. What are you doing in here on your day off?" she asked her. Alice sat Lottie at a nearby table with her colouring book and pens while she slowly walked with Alfie, holding both his hands as he took wobbly steps into the tearoom. "Maya asked me to meet her here," said Alice, giving Maggie a peck on the cheek to say hello. "She said she had an important announcement."

"Oh, right" Said Maggie. "She has booked a family table. I wonder what it's all about." She picked up Alfie, who had tired of walking, and took him over to the terrace to point out the swans and seagulls to him. There were no other customers yet. The early morning dog walkers had been and gone, and it was not quite time for the morning cream tea brigade. Alfie saw Maya and Freddie arriving before Maggie did, and alerted her by calling for "Weddie" in his adorable little voice. She turned in the direction he was looking and was surprised to see Maya walking in with her mum and dad and Oliver Anderson. Freddie was enjoying a ride on Oliver' shoulders, and Maggie couldn't be sure, but it looked as though Oliver were holding the boy's legs with one hand and holding Maya's hand with the other. She tried to call Alice to draw her attention to it, but Lottie beat her too it, running to the gate to greet Maya with a bear hug to the legs.

Maggie directed them to the table she had prepared, and they all sat down. Alice joined them with Lottie and Alfie, and they were all deep in conversation by the time Maggie went over to take their order. "Maggie, can you join us?" said Maya. "Can one of your waitresses take our order? You should be a part of this." Maggie looked nervously between Maya and Pamela, unsure how to answer. Pamela nodded "Its ok Maggie. Please join us. Maya has something she would like to say."

"Well ok then," said Maggie smiling. She waved a waitress over and took a seat between Alice and Oliver. She and Alice exchanged look, trying to work out what was going on between Oliver and Maya. It was clear the two of them were at least dating, but they couldn't work out how deep the relationship ran. Once they were all tucking into strawberry scones and earl grey tea Maya raised a hand to get everyone's attention. "Hey, everyone.... friends and family..." she began, uncharacteristically nervous. "I asked you all here today because I'm sick of the secrets. I can't keep things secret anymore, it's been eating away at me for years without me even realising, so here goes" She took a deep breath and looked at Oliver, addressing everything toward him. "Oliver is Freddie's Dad. We had a one-night thing and Oliver didn't know, but Freddie was born. I didn't say anything because Oliver was still with his wife at the time, but now he knows he would like to be part of Freddie's life, and I want you all to welcome him to the family." She smiled and took his hand. He beamed back at her and it seemed that they only had eyes for each other. There was an awkward silence around the table as people tried to decide if it was appropriate to speak. Maggie was first to speak. "I think that's amazing..."

"That's not all" interrupted Maya, "Oliver is not the only new member of the family." This time she smiled at Maggie. "So, it seems I was not the only one keeping secrets," She shot a fake look of annoyance at her Mother. "Maggie is my half-sister and Freddie's Aunty" Alice's hands flew to her mouth as she gasped her surprise while Maggie looked at Pamela to check that she was ok with the revelation. Pamela smiled reassuringly. Maya continued. "Maggie, I am so pleased to have you in my life and I intend to make up for every second we have lost up until now." She leaned across the table and wrapped her arms around her. "My sister Maggie," she whispered into Maggie's hair. "I like the sound of that." Maggie kissed Maya on the cheek and sat back in the chair, not knowing quite how to respond. Alice put a hand on her arm, pulling her in for a hug. "I can't believe you never said anything." She shook her head, a big grin on her face. "I'm so pleased for you." Maggie hugged her back, grinning from ear to ear.

Everyone around the table was smiling and chatting about what they had just heard. Alice teased Maya, "So does this mean that you and Oliver are dating now?" She laughed. Maya glanced at Oliver, but before she had a chance to answer Pamela called for their attention. She looked downcast, wringing her hands below the table, "Erm, while everyone is all together, I have another thing to say, but I'm afraid I'm going to spoil the mood."

"What is it Mum?" said Maya, suddenly concerned.

"I had a hospital appointment yesterday... with an oncologist." She hesitated and looked at the faces around the table. She closed her eyes "I have liver Cancer. Advanced liver Cancer." Graham took her hand and smiled sadly at her, nodding to encourage her to continue. Pamela returned his nod, seeming to gain strength from him. "I have about two weeks to live." There were several small gasps around the table, Pamela shook her head. "No, no, no, you don't get to be sad about this. We have finally come together as a family and we have this short time to make the most of it." She looked at Maggie. "Maggie. My daughter. I'm so sorry for how I have treated you. For forcing you to keep my secret. It was unfair and cruel of me to keep you from your Sister."

"It's ok" Said Maggie, tears in her eyes. "I understand why you did it. I just wish I had longer with you."

"And Maya" continued Pamela, smiling at her daughter. "My darling girl. I have watched you grow into a beautiful woman and a fantastic mother. I couldn't be prouder of you. You have brought nothing but joy to me and your father." She smiled at Graham and kissed his hand. "And you have given us the most adorable Grandbaby that anyone ever had," her voice cracked. She couldn't continue speaking. Alice stood up and took over. "Ok, my turn. This party needs cheering up a bit." She grinned and was rewarded with a smattering of laughs. "I know I am not officially family. But you know what, I couldn't think of a family I would rather call my own. Every single person around this table has been there for me when I needed help. I have never been judged by you and have felt nothing but love from all of you. So, from now I am adopting you all as surrogate family for me and my children. So there" She sat down with a thump and raised her teacup in a toast. "To family."

"To family," everyone responded, raising their teacups and clinking them together. The children laughed, not understanding what was going on, but enjoying the atmosphere.

"Well, I think this has turned into a celebration" Maggie called the nearest waitress over. "We need Champagne. Lots of Champagne" The waitress nodded and hurried off to get the drinks.

The party continued through lunch and into the afternoon, with everyone building bonds and deepening friendships with each other that would last a lifetime.

CHAPTER 35
MAGGIE 2019

Maggie wiped a tear away with her hand and held her breathe, doing her best to control her emotions. When Maya had asked her to say a few words at their Mother's funeral, she had been honoured, but she hadn't realised just how hard it would hit her. She looked out from the podium across a sea of faces. The image swam in her head, and she wondered for a second if she was going to throw up. She had barely introduced herself and now she was frozen to the spot. She picked up the poem she had written with shaky hands, but she couldn't bring herself to read it.

Maggie felt someone take her hand and was grateful to see that Maya had joined her up on the stage. Her half-sister took the poem from her hand and read it aloud. She then walked with Maggie over to the coffin and placed the poem among the white lilies that were arranged there. Maggie picked up a white rose and laid it gently next to the poem, before resting her hand lightly on the coffin and saying a silent goodbye. She had not been a part of Pamela's life for very long, but in just a few short weeks she had got to know her as well as was possible in the circumstances. She had finally found the thing that she had been craving her whole life. A family.

As the funeral ended Maggie and Maya left hand in hand. They were met at the front of the chapel by Alice, who hugged them both in turn. "It was a beautiful service." Maya squeezed her hand and flashed her a sad smile. "It really was. She would have been pleased to see everyone here." She straightened her jacket, visibly shaking off her sadness. "Right. Pub time." Maggie grinned and echoed her sister. "Pub time it is." The three of them crunched across the gravel driveway, into the waiting limos that had been hired to drive them to the wake. They fell silent on the drive, and as she sat quietly in the back of the car between her best friend and her sister, Maggie reflected on recent events. Here she was, exactly a year after Daniel's funeral and her life had changed beyond recognition. Daniel would have been thrilled for her. He had understood her need for family more than anyone she had ever known. She said a silent goodbye to him in her head, acknowledging her sadness at losing him for the first time. She realised she had never cried for him or mourned him in any way, too afraid to face those feelings. Finally she felt safe enough to let herself grieve for everything she had lost.

Maya was the first to break the silence as the car drew up alongside the pub. "Oh, there's Oli." She gathered her things onto her lap and jumped out of the car as soon as it stopped, running up to Oliver and hugging him tightly before leading him by the hand through the entrance. Maggie smiled. The made a lovely couple. The two of them had planned to take things slowly, but within just a few short days they had realised they were deeply in love with each other. Maya told Maggie that she had loved Oliver from the moment they had met and since having Freddie that feeling had just grown. She had never so much as dated another man, no one had ever lived up to Oliver in her mind.

A friend of Maya's had been watching Freddie, Lottie and Alfie for them. The three children were waiting for them in the pub garden, where they were playing in a huge tree house. Oliver let go of Maya's hand, gave her a kiss on the cheek, and joined the children in their games. He was a fantastic father to Freddie, and the boy had already formed a close bond with him. Maggie glanced at Maya, who was watching the two men in her life playing together with obvious love in her eyes. She must have sensed Maggie watching her, as without moving her head she spoke, "I wish I hadn't waited so long to tell him, Mags. They love each other so much. He could have been there for Freddie when he was sick." She took a sip of the gin and tonic that Alice had just placed in front of her. "Most of the time I was too tired to help him, you know. He should have had his father there by his side. It was my selfish fault he was alone." Maggie took a sip of her own drink and traced her finger through the condensation that had pooled on the table in a circle. "I don't think it matters." She turned to face Maya who had a quizzical look on her face. "It doesn't matter what happened in the past. You did the best thing you could back then according to your circumstances. I don't think you should let that matter now." Maya set her drink down on the table. "What are you talking about? Of course the past matters. I'm saying if Freddie had known his Dad things would have been better." Maggie covered Maya's hand with her own. "Yes, maybe it would," she said calmly. "But he didn't. And that's ok too. All the things that happened in the past had to happen the way they did, to get us to where we are now. And I happen to think that place it pretty good." She smiled at the two women. "So, it doesn't matter that some of it was bad. It's the difficult stuff that makes us grow." Maggie could see Alice nodding out of the corner of her eye. "Life is good right now, at this very moment. And we need to be thankful for that and enjoy it. And yes, things may become difficult again in the future, and if they do, we will worry about that then. Together." Alice smiled and added her hand to the pile on top of Maya and Maggie's. "Amen to that."

Printed in Great Britain
by Amazon